THE BIDDULPH PLAYERS

1950 - 2000

"NEED ONE SUFFER SO MUCH FOR PLEASURE"

Margaret Fernyhough, Doris Page and Elisabeth Lawton

CHURNET VALLEY BOOKS
Leek, Staffordshire. 01538 399033
email: picture.book@virgin.net web: freespace.virgin.net/c.hinton/

ISBN 1 897949 67 7

INTRODUCTION

A few years ago Doris Page compiled a potted history of Biddulph Players and read it out to members at the A.G.M. After the meeting Peter Averill sent Doris some missing programmes to add to her collection and work began on making a list of the plays performed since the formation of the society.

I thought it would be a good idea to have copies made to sell to interested members, but the history idea then lay dormant and forgotten for several years in a computer. After the funeral of Alice Ashton, the wife of our founder John, her daughter Judith Hollies invited members back to her home and we were able to look through Alice's scrapbook. The photographs we saw there aroused our interest in the history once again.

My sister Elisabeth Lawton had compiled a History of Brown Edge which was published in 1998 by Churnet Valley Books, and she encouraged Doris and myself to approach the same publisher with her, and they agreed to take it on. We set the date of the Golden Anniversary of Biddulph Players, May 2000, for publication - and as it was now November 1999, the work began in earnest.

With Doris's original potted history as a framework, I set out to catalogue all the plays chronologically, to find photographs for nearly all of them and to bring together a series of little cameo pieces by members. I have sought to show the hard work and the fun involved, and hopefully to produce a fascinating record of the past 50 years both for the members to enjoy but also for a wider audience. As well as a cast list I have tried to attach a newspaper extract to every play which along with the photograph may help other amateur societies in choosing their plays. I also hope that the book will make the public more aware of our society - and that with any luck we will also raise some money, through sales, for the Building Fund.

Despite the fact that so many amateur dramatic societies are struggling to survive, I am very confident that the dedication of many of our members will take the Players forward into the new century.

Margaret Fernyhough, Editor

CONTENTS

John Ashton as he appeared in "The Devil a Saint", 1938. John is seated right.

John Ashton as he appeared in "White Secrets" 1938.

Alice in "The Gondoliers" 1938.

JOHN ASHTON, FOUNDER OF BIDDULPH PLAYERS A.D.S. and ALICE ASHTON

by Judith Hollies

My parents were born in the small Lancashire mill town of Todmorden at the beginning of the twentieth century. They came from very different backgrounds. My father had a lousy childhood and little schooling. When he was just two his father died and his maternal grandmother moved the whole of her extended family over to America. His mother remarried and returned to England with her second, Todmorden-born, husband. John was just nine and endured many a thrashing in school for not being able to calculate in pounds, shillings and pence. At thirteen he started work.

John Ashton as a young man.

His step-father was a violent man who one night turned them both out into the street without even a toothbrush. How John and his mother fared that night I don't know but for many years afterwards John nursed his ailing mother. It must have been a solitary and miserable start to life but I know my father had a love of reading and a ready and quirky wit. He loved to make people laugh. When he met my mother he spent many a happy hour in their house at Bank Top.

My maternal grandfather, James Hollows Fielden, held a white-collar job in the cotton mill. It meant security and a middle-class lifestyle for his seven children, of whom my mother was the youngest. In those days, as my mother was so fond of telling me, they made their own amusement. My mother learned to play the piano and the violin. Her sister Florence had a celebrated soprano voice and sang all over the country at concerts and festivals. Being eleven years older than my mother, she preceded her on to the stage in local amateur dramatic and operatic productions and little Alice grew up principally amidst productions of Gilbert and Sullivan, of which she remained a devotee all of her life. But, whilst Flo had the voice, Alice had the drama and in this she excelled.

Alice Fielden as Mme. Rabelais in "High Jinks"

Across the road from her home at Bank Top stood the Unitarian Church. In her teens Alice spent most of her time there. Was she very religious you ask? Not at all. The fact was, all the social activities for the community were generated by the church. Dances, fetes, drama, musical evenings, whist drives; she even conducted the children's choir. Her thirst for treading the boards and her flair for organisation was seemingly unquenchable.

She met my father through his cousin Frank, whom she courted for a short time, and every evening John would wait in the wings for Alice to finish the production in hand or the

John and Alice Ashton in "The Skin Game". John is centre with Alice seated right c.1937.

T L T

The Todmorden Little Theatre

presents

"The Skin Game"

A Tragi-Comedy in 3 Acts

By John Galsworthy

(Under Licence from the League of British Dramatists).

COSTUMES and WIGS by S. B. Watts and Co., Manchester.

SCENERY by the Little Theatre.

STAGE FURNITURE by Little Theatre and Todmorden Co-operative Society.

LIGHTING by the Little Theatre.

rehearsal in progress. Would she never give it up? Obviously not. The phrase, "If you can't lick 'em join 'em," wasn't coined back then but very aptly describes my father's predicament. At last Alice persuaded him to join the Little Todmorden Theatre. He joined the ranks of amateur actors and caught the 'acting bug'. He was hooked. They married in 1934 in the Unitarian Church and appeared in several plays together before moving to Biddulph some time in 1939.

My father was helped in getting a job as a hospital porter at Biddulph Grange Hospital. At that time Biddulph Grange was owned by Lancashire County Council and my mother's brother-in-law was a councillor. My father moved down first, finding a suitable house to rent, and my mother followed just before Christmas. She was desperately homesick. Behind her she had left a large family, a host of friends and a way of life that could not be replicated. It was a dismal and lonely Christmas.

During the following year, ever gregarious, my mother talked to people at the bus-stop, at work, in the shops and made friends with anyone who would talk back. She even invited soldiers to share Christmas dinner with them. But it wasn't enough and it wasn't home. Then they had me. Just where and when the idea for the beginning of a dramatic society took place I do not know. But the friends my mother had succeeded in making were now probably exerting some influence. With one of these, a Londoner called Bill Beadle, my father went round knocking on doors, asking if anyone would be interested in starting a dramatic society. The response was enough to make a start and the society was formed in 1949.

Alice Fielden as Rachel Pym in
"The Quaker Girl" 1933

Alice(second left) with her sisters.

Knypersley Youth Club drama group c.1960.
Left to right: Muriel Evans, Malcolm Locker, Christine Sherratt, Ruth Burton, Pamela Brough, John Ashton

Knypersley Youth Club drama group c.1958. Christine Worsley, Pauline Ault, John Oakes, Geoffrey Gidman, Malcolm Locker, Sheila Bennison, Betty Holland.

John Ashton produced 37 plays to entertain the people of Biddulph. His high standard of production was achieved by attention to detail and a discipline tempered by a dry humour, a fine appreciation of the essence of a play and in comedy a great sense of timing.

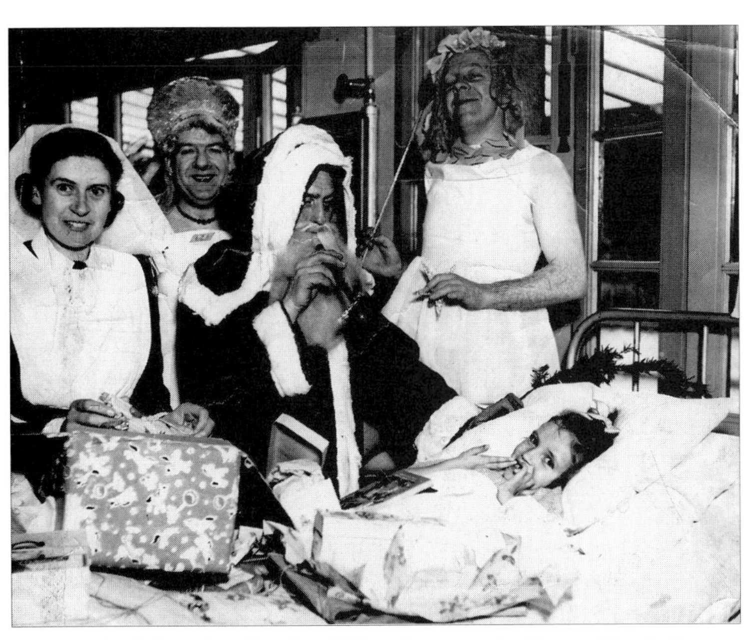

John Ashton keeping the children happy at the Grange Hospital.

In the early sixties Malcolm Locker invited John to help out with the Knypersley Youth Club Drama Group. Some of the members of this group went on to become stalwart members of Biddulph Players. Malcolm recalls how he and John attended a drama workshop at Bangor in North Wales. The lecturer, a director of "Oh What a Lovely War", was so impressed with John and asked what he did for a living, When Malcolm said he was a hospital porter the reply was "What a waste of talent".

Not really, he came to live in Biddulph and started a drama group, still going strong after fifty years. What greater memorial or legacy could he have than this. He produced his last play in 1975 and died in 1979 at the age of 78 years.

John Ashton c1970

Alice Ashton as we remember her

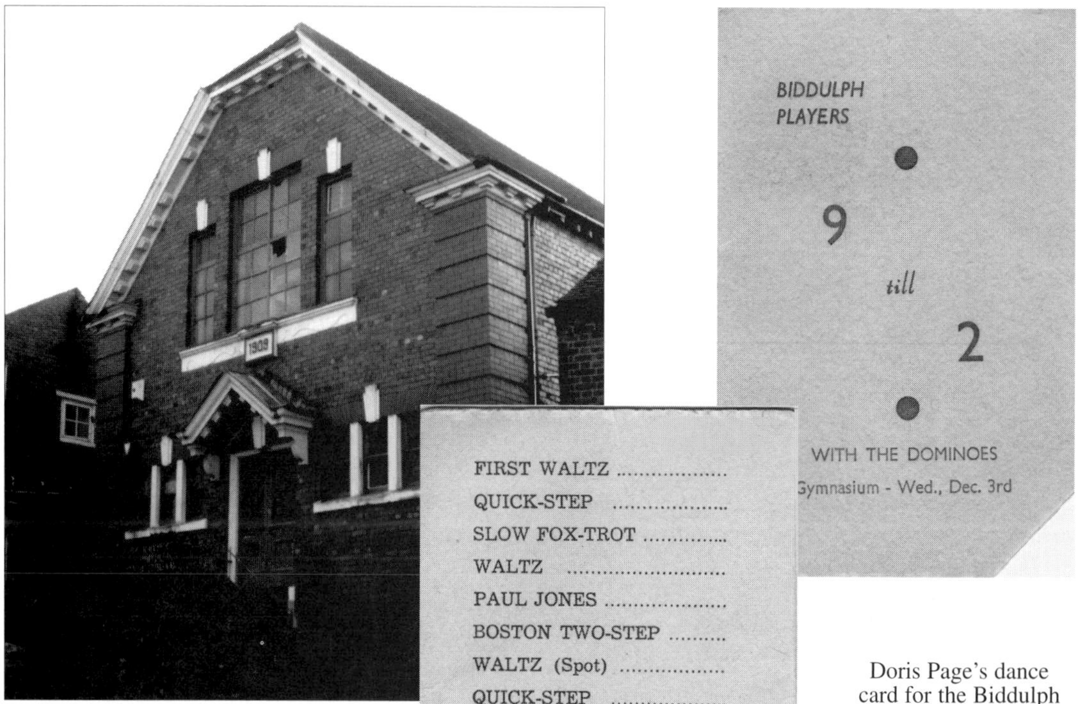
BIDDULPH
PLAYERS
9
till
2
WITH THE DOMINOES
Gymnasium - Wed., Dec. 3rd

FIRST WALTZ ....
QUICK-STEP ....
SLOW FOX-TROT ....
WALTZ ....
PAUL JONES ....
BOSTON TWO-STEP ....
WALTZ (Spot) ....
QUICK-STEP ....
SLOW FOX-TROT ....
ST. BERNARD WALTZ ......
QUICK-STEP ....

Interval

QUICK-STEP ....
WALTZ ....
OLD TYME MEDLEY ....

The Gymnasium in Wharf Road, venue for the first twenty one productions of Biddulph Players. It was donated to the people of Biddulph by Robert Heath in 1909 and is still owned by the Conservative Club and used for Martial Arts.

Doris Page's dance card for the Biddulph Players dance 1953.

Members of the social committee at the Players' dance at the Gymnasium 1953.
Standing: Peter Averill, Harold Whalley, Harry Morris, Douglas Brown, Archie Averill.
Seated: Jean Jones, Cynthia Brown, Janet Millward, Megan Porter, Cyril Millward.

A POTTED HISTORY OF BIDDULPH PLAYERS PART I: 1950-1963 GYMNASIUM

Doris Page

In 1949 a notice appeared in the Biddulph Chronicle stating that a Mr John Ashton wished to start a drama group in Biddulph. Anyone interested was asked to attend a meeting to be held in the Conservative Club in the High Street.

When I arrived at the meeting I found 30 to 40 people seated in the main body of the hall with another twenty people facing them. The people at the front were the ones whom John had already spoken to beforehand. They were in the main not interested in acting but were prepared to stand for office and committee work. I only knew about two of them by sight which made it difficult when we were asked to vote for them.

I was elected onto the social committee, whose aim was to raise money for our productions. Our account was to be called "The Social and Building Fund" - we hoped eventually to raise enough funds for our own theatre. It was decided that our official title would be "The Biddulph Players Amateur Dramatic Society". However we would be known as `Biddulph Players' and we would put on three plays a year.

Doris in her 'Gymnasium' days.

John was not interested in acting himself; his 'forte' was directing. He seemed to see movements in his mind's eye when he read the script. I feel he really missed his vocation in life. He agreed to direct two of the plays each year and any other interested member could do the third one. As things worked out we usually staged two comedies and one straight play, a murder or drama.

The first task for the members was to select the play - the right play - for our first production. We met weekly for play readings. I remember one that we read was called "The Skin Game", which I was very impressed with.

We eventually decided on a comedy by Eynon Evans entitled "Wishing Well". The action takes place in a room of the `Wishing Well' 'a guest house in the Welsh countryside. The guests include a disagreeable married couple, a lady of means and a war widow who has not recovered from the blow of losing her husband killed in action. Thanks to the proprietor of the guest house and the village postman a marvellous change occurs in the outlook of the guests towards their problems. I played the part of the young niece of the landlord, Delith Gwyn.

We used different venues for our first rehearsals, namely the school hall in Gunn Street, the social hut in Heath Street and various members' homes. I think the first play was financed by the subscriptions that we paid. This was ordinary members 5/- and Vice-Presidents, (these are now called patrons) 10/-. A dance was held at the Gymnasium on December the 6th to raise more funds, (this building is now the Karate Club). The tickets were priced at 5/- inclusive and it was 8pm until 1am to a live band. When I look at the old programmes I am surprised at the number of dances we did hold in addition to the annual one.

The date for the play was to be 19th to the 22nd April 1950 and it was to be held at the Gymnasium. I remember, as the date of the play loomed, we were all suffering from nerves. We could only have the hall for our rehearsals from the Friday previous to the play. We had no 'props' or flats as we know them now and no curtains that really fitted. The stage was nothing more than a glorified platform. The men made a stage `apron' to give it some depth, utilising old ammunition boxes they had found in someone's garage. They first had to break them open, and then they made trestles and boards to go across the top.

I believe the set took about 14-15 hours to build each time, but I imagine this depended on how many helpers were there. We had so little room back stage; if a player exited stage right, they had to stay there until the interval or the end, unless of course we altered the script or the stage directions. The men used to crawl underneath the stage but needless to say the ladies were not too keen on this manoeuvre. I remember one play when the maid exited right and then later re-appeared and, without saying a word, wandered across the stage, and off left. It transpired that the cue for her entrance had been missed. She knew that the doorbell was going to ring and had to announce someone stage left.

However I digress - the first play. The hero was in a wheelchair and I, dressed as a bridesmaid, had to wheel him in. There was no one to help me and, owing to the lack of space, it was a real struggle. I was glad that the audience did not hear the comments from the wheelchair when his knee came into contact with the doorframe. I entered like someone from the wreck of the 'Hesperus' with my head-dress over one eye and my cape over one shoulder. I was told that we didn't look as bad as we felt but I shall always have my doubts.

The hall was only half full on the Wednesday, but the audience must have enjoyed it because we had a few more people every night. We even had to put extra seats out on the Saturday night. The hall held about 100 chairs but we still had to turn some people away.

The back-stage workers were:

Stage manager - Keith Nixon
Properties - Frances Dean
Prompters - Margaret Ashley, Betty Connor
Scenery - Enid Stoddard
Business Manager - Cyril Millward
Booking plan - Janet Millward

Janet used to draw a plan of the seating and the cast were given first choice. The tickets were sold at Machin's Outfitters in the High Street, now occupied by the Cheshire Building Society. We had proper tickets printed by the local printer, Hagston, who also did the programmes and posters. I think the prices of the tickets were Wednesday 2/6 Thursday and Friday 3/- and Saturday 4/-. Later the pre-booking of tickets was only available on Saturdays and was eventually discontinued . By 1969 the prices had risen to 3/-, 3/6 and 4/-.

Our first officials were: Chairman - Alfred T Rogers; Treasurer - William Beadle; Secretary - Frances Dean. We did not choose a President at our first meeting but by 1951 it was Major (later Colonel) Lovatt.

We had no props of our own and in this department we will always be indebted to Mr John Garside for the help he gave us. His shop is still in Biddulph in the High Street, opposite the cenotaph. He used to lend us brand new suites of furniture, tables, chairs, lamps. Anything we asked for, if he had it we could borrow it. He was also the local undertaker, but we did not bother him in that direction, I'm pleased to say.

I remember on many occasions we were unable to start our dress rehearsal on Tuesday night until after 9 pm. This was because members were dashing around still locating props needed for the play. We had to go right through the script as it was our first time on the stage, and I remember once we did not leave the Gym until 1.00am.

The next two plays that first season were "Young Mrs Barrington" and "Grand National Night". We continued at the Gym for a number of years putting three plays on nearly every season. There were not many occasions when we only did two.

In 1951 we were asked to put on an extra play for the Festival of Britain celebrations. We chose "When We are Married" and even put on a matinee performance for the pensioners on Saturday afternoon. It was a really hot summer and I remember it was very distracting because we could see the audience. There was no way of blacking out the hall. Some of the older members of the audience could remember back to the style of the clothes we were wearing, and the way the set was furnished, and we could hear all sorts of comments.

When Park Lane estate was being built, one of our members, Peter Averill, became friendly with some of the workmen, several of whom joined the Players. We had electricians, fitters, joiners and painters. They helped us build the proscenium arch and better flats. I have a feeling that a lot of the materials used came courtesy of `Costains'. Whether Mr Costain was aware of this arrangement shall remain their secret.

We bought brown velvet stage curtains, which are still in use in our clubroom. As you can imagine these items all enhanced greatly the appearance of our stage.

At this time we had collected a few bits of furniture and props and the question of storage became an important issue. The trestles went under the stage at the Gym - I have often wondered if they are still there. We first hired the cellar of the `Bird in Hand' public house in Station Road. Later Baileys (now Butlers) let us have a dusty old loft at the back of their premises. I think the Players put a new door in the wall in Albert Street, and everything had to be lowered onto the lorry. When Butlers took over we were no longer able to use these premises. Other places of storage included a garage belonging to Alan and Mary Hart, and a disused building belonging to Biddulph Moor church. It was during this period that a lot of our things were spoilt by rainwater, and others went missing.

The fetching and carrying entailed a lot of hard work. We will always be grateful for the help of Mr Hulme, who loaned us his coal lorry. We could never have managed without it. Other helpers at this time were Dave Jerrard, Alf Wilshaw and Jack Machin, who helped us to move the flats and did other chores. The electricians who assisted were Eric Podmore, Arnold Goodwin, Lewis Chaddock, Roy Barlow and Robert Shaw.

In 1963 we left the Gymnasium and moved to a new venue - a new era was set to begin.

THE ACTION OF THE PLAY TAKES PLACE IN THE LOUNGE OF THE WISHING WELL INN

ACT I.

Four o'clock in the afternoon of a Spring Day

ACT II.

Scene 1—A few days later

Scene 2—The following day

ACT III.

Scene 1—A few days later

Scene 2—About a month later. Saturday afternoon.

Time—The Present.

Officials of the Biddulph Players—

Chairman	ALFRED T. ROGERS
Hon. Treasurer	WILLIAM BEADLE
Hon. Secretary	FRANCES M. DEAN
Stage Manager	KEITH NIXON
Stage Assistants	CYRIL MOSS, STANLEY BENTLEY
Lights and Effects	ERIC PODMORE
Properties	FRANCES M. DEAN
Scenery	ENID STANNARD
Prompters	MARJORIE P. ASHLEY, BETTY CANNON
Business Manager	CYRIL MILLWARD

Booking Plan kindly undertaken by Janet R. Millward.

"WISHING WELL"

by E. EYNON EVANS

CAST (in order of appearance)

JANE (The Housekeeper at the Wishing Well)	BETTY LOVATT
JOHN PUGH (Henry's Grandson)	PETER AVERILL
ABNER (An old villager)	PETER EVERALL
HENRY PUGH (Landlord of the Wishing Well)	HARRY CARTHY
DELITH GWYN (Henry's niece)	DORIS PAGE
AMOS PARRY (The village Postman)	SAM REEVES
AMELIA SMITH (a visitor)	MOLLIE CARTWRIGHT
MORGAN MORGAN (her chauffeur)	HAROLD WHALLEY
PETER JENNINGS (visitors)	FRED DIXON
IRENE JENNINGS (visitors)	SYLVIA MOSS
ANN MURRAY (visitors)	DOROTHY PEASEGOOD

PRODUCED BY JOHN ASHTON

First production "Wishing Well" programme.

The set of "Wishing Well".

"Wishing Well".
Harry Carthy, John Ashton (producer), Fred Dixon, Peter Everall, Sam Reeves, Harold Whalley.
Seated: Peter Averill, Betty Lovatt, Dorothy Peasegood, Doris Page, Sylvia Moss, Mollie Cartwright.

NOTABLE SUCCESS IN FIRST PRODUCTION

"The Biddulph Players presented their first play in Biddulph Gymnasium for four nights last week and achieved a notable success. There were full bookings for all performances and on the final presentation on Saturday night many were disappointed at not being able to gain admission. The players chose Wishing Well a comedy in three acts by Eynon Williams.

The play is not lacking in emotional interest , and as the landlord's grandson crippled in the war, Peter Averill played a creditable part.

The players acted with sincerity and considerable ability, and splendid performances in the chief roles were given by Harry Carthy, the landlord and Sam Reeves, the village postman.

Enid Stannard was responsible for the scenery and Francis M Dean for the properties and they are to be congratulated upon their work. The stage had been prepared down to the last detail - even to the provision of a copy of a Welsh newspaper. Their work was enhanced by the lighting effects arranged by Mr Eric Podmore. John Ashton is to be congratulated on his production of the play."

Harry Carthy

Harry Carthy took on the role of the Welsh landlord of the "Wishing Well". He went to the first meeting in response to John Ashton's advert, little realising he would be given a major role. He had to learn an immense number of lines and adopt a Welsh accent. It was fortunate that his wife was Welsh and able to help him.

He took on numerous roles in those early years and also helped backstage as stage manager and assistant electrician. His favourite play was the amusing and brilliant "When We Are Married" by J.B.Priestley. He also helped to design and construct the first switchboard to control the stage lighting.

"The Young Mrs Barrington"
Peter Averill, Joan Basson, Megan Porter, Cynthia Brown, Douglas Brown.

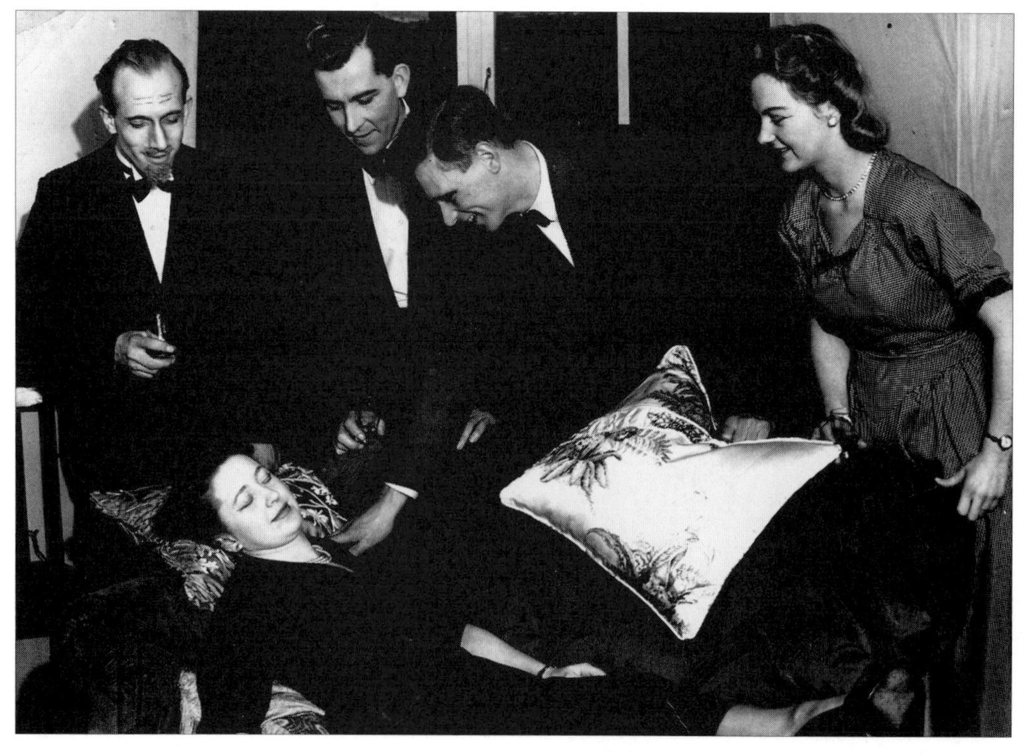

"Grand National Night"
Standing: Harry Carthy, Peter Averill, Len Lee, Joan Lee. Reclining: Barbara Copeland.

"The Blue Goose"
Standing: Len Lee, Mollie Cartwright, Frank Gaulton , Peter Averill, Reg Yates, Sam Reeves, Sylvia Moss.
Seated: Jean Lee, Cynthia Brown, Joan Basson.

"When the mayor forgets his worries and his carefully prepared speech - under the influence of a hot posset."

"Special mention must be made of the stage and setting which would do credit to many a professional company. Backstage activities are screened by a magnificent proscenium".

Joan Basson

"And some of the performances - notably that of Joan Basson, as the borough treasurer's wife - infuse life and humour into lines not noticeably imbued with either quality. Mrs Basson's portrayal is, indeed, the strong centre-piece around which the play is firmly built. As the butter-fly minded Mrs Portal, she displays an acute sense of timing, variety in her tone inflections, and a singing voice whose quality belies the suggestion - by another member of the cast - that a piccolo is needed to take her top notes for her".

"When We Are Married"
Standing: Harry Morris, Sam Reeves, Harry Carthy, Peter Averill, Barbara Copeland, Megan Porter, Mollie Cartwright, Fred Dixon
Seated: Eleanor Averill, Cynthia Brown, Betty Lovatt, Doris Page, Douglas Brown, Harold Whalley.

"When We Are Married" - Festival of Britain production

"Three married couples celebrating their silver wedding discover they are not really married, due to the parson's error. The stage is lavishly set with heavy furniture, antimacassars, rugs, what-nots, palms, old family portraits and pictures, and various other impedimentia of the period. The Players are to be congratulated, for not having a `home' of their own they have to carry their props round with them, as it were, and during productions transform the small stage at the Gymnasium into quite a spacious setting, managing quite admirably with the meagre staging and dressing arrangements.

Most of the cast are required to maintain Yorkshire accents throughout the play, and here again the Players are to be congratulated. As Joseph Helliwell, the head of the household, Sam Reeves is excellent. With clever movements and facial expressions he portrays the typical Yorkshireman. The difficult part of Councillor Albert Parker is ably maintained by Harry Carthy. Completing the male triangle is plain Mr. Herbert Soppitt. He is played with a modicum of movement and a dead-pan expression by Harry Morris, who excels as the henpecked husband.

The wives are as contrasting in character as their husbands: the quiet, the normal and the nagging. Maria Helliwell is played by Cynthia Brown. The part is very capably handled, and the scene where she presents the household keys, books and badly-needed darning to her husband's blousy ex-girlfriend is most amusing. Annie Parker, the quiet one is charmingly acted by Betty Lovatt. Poor Herbert Soppitt is married to a real tartar called Clara (played by Eleanor Averill), who nags and screams at him throughout the whole proceedings but is eventually subdued and dumbfounded when he finally puts her in her place.

Romance is provided by Peter Averill as Gerald Forbes, local chapel organist, and Doris Page as Nancy Holmes, Alderman and Mrs Helliwell's quiet neice. Two excellent character studies are given by Megan Porter as the cheeky maid, Ruby Birtle, and Mollie Cartwright as Mrs Northrop, the daily, who overhears the conversations through the keyhole and provides an hilarious scene when she breaks the disastrous news to the wives. The reporter from the `Argus' is played by Douglas Brown, and Henry Ormanroid, the photographer who becomes more inebriated as the evening wears on, is a clever piece of acting by Fred Dixon. Completing the cast are Barbara Copeland as Lottie Grady the ex-barmaid and Harold Whalley as the Reverend Clement Mercer, both of whom are excellently cast. The play is capably produced by John Ashton."

"All the World's a Stage."

Peter Averill

From acting to producing a play was a tremendous shock to the system. As an actor I was expected to assume a character, learn the lines and remember the moves. As a producer I was expected to help the actors create the character, know virtually every character's lines and plan all movements. In addition, scenery, props, lighting, sound effects, stage-managing, etc., all had to be organised, entailing continual liason with all the people responsible for each of these tasks.

But all of this comes after picking the play with the selection committee. We had to decide whether it would be comedy or drama (I found it much easier to produce drama), the appeal it would have to the audience and the availability of people for the parts. One of the problems all producers had in those days was the shortage of male actors, and plays had to be selected accordingly.

Once the play and the players had been chosen, one of the problems to producer and actors alike was the lack of a stage to rehearse on and props and scenery to go with it. The basement of the Gymnasium and people's homes were part of many imaginary sets. Rehearsals were twice a week and often producers had planned a scene or act for a particular evening only to be frustrated by the major player in that particular act or scene being ill or having a last minute commitment. This resulted in the players who did attend having to rehearse small parts of more than one scene.

The first time on stage was the dress rehearsal, often accompanied by the sound of hammers, saws and pieces of furniture being moved around. The temptation to change moves was always very strong but had to be resisted to avoid chaos, unless the move was very minor and giving a more dramatic effect to the whole scene. Nevertheless changes had to be made and, as Doris Page says midnight oil often burned at dress rehearsals.

Opening night was the time that producers and back-stage team indulged in drinks or tranquillisers when, due to nerves, some of the actors forgot their lines or made wrong entrances or exits and, on one memorable occasion leapt from Act 1 to Act 3 giving myself, the stage managers and the prompter apoplexy!

Despite all this, it was great fun and I enjoyed every minute of the thirteen years I was part of Biddulph Players and made a lot of lasting friendships.

Congratulations and long may you continue.

"Set in a North London paper shop. The jealous lover Charlie, son of the proprietor murders his ex-girlfriend Bella. The consequences of his deed are not unforseen but the producer, John Ashton, in his presentation keeps the entire audience in suspense until the end."

"Heaven and Charing Cross"
Standing: Barbara Copeland, Douglas Brown, Jean Jones, Peter Averill, Doris Page, Lucy Milnes, Ted Averill, Hyam Bailey.
Seated: Harry Carthy, Betty Lovatt, Eleanor Averill, Sylvia Moss.

Douglas Brown

Douglas first appeared on stage in the concerts put on at the Church Hall (now Saxon Tyres). He saw the production of "Wishing Well" and went along to the reading of the second play, "Young Mrs. Barrington," taking on the part of Arthur Barrington. He remembers very vividly his entrance through the french windows, swinging the chicken and saying his line *"Chicken for dinner tomorrow girls"*.

During another scene in the play, which involved a fishing rod, he trod on the line and the hook became embedded in his foot. Fortunately for Douglas, Dr. Miller was in the audience and came backstage to help. Several lines had to be cut out of the script before the good doctor administered first aid and Douglas could return to the stage.

"A comedy set in the living room of Hill Top Farm, the home of the Weatherheads, in the village of Upper Netherwick."

"Without the Prince"
Standing: Ted Averill, Arthur Gibson, Dorothy Peasegood, Douglas Brown, Harry Morris, Frank Gaulton, Mollie Cartwright.
Seated: Lucy Milnes, Harold Whalley, Jean Jones.

An army officer, thought to have died a hero's death at Caen, returns as a coward who deserted his post in the face of danger.

"The opening performance (though not a paragon of all virtues) had that virtue, supremely important in amateur dramatics - a refreshing clarity of diction."

The set of **"The Paragon"**. The study of Sir Rawley's house.

A Players' New Year's Eve party held at the `Biddulph Arms' in the early 1950s.

Young widow, having clandestine love affair with the son of the family, arrives at their home and all is revealed.

"In the title role John Longman, a Canadian residing in the Biddulph district, makes his first appearance with the Players. He was admirably suited for the role, and gave an excellent performance, supported by an able cast."

"The Good Young Man"
Standing: Arthur Gibson, Eleanor Averill, John Longman, Harry Morris, Donald Baskeyfield. Seated: Margaret Clowes, Barbara Copeland, Doris Page.

"And all the men and women in it merely players"

Kathleen Thomas

Biddulph Players figured in my life from my very early teens. I was taken by my parents, Mr and Mrs Maurice Rowley, to every play, always for the evening performance on Saturday. In those days some of the young people, including myself, were chosen to present a bouquet of flowers to each lady member of the cast on the last night. At that age, 14-15 years old, ,it was so exciting and something we really looked forward to. Sometimes we couldn't wait for the play to end so we could do 'our part'! When I came to tread the boards myself that part of the proceedings had bitten the dust - what a shame!

All my friends and members of my family were associated with the society in some capacity or another and most of my social life (end of play parties, New Year's Eve parties, 'any excuse' parties) was centred around the Players. My Daddy was the Chairman of the society, my Uncle Cyril (Millward) was the house manager and my Auntie Janet (Millward) sold tickets from her shop in the High Street. On top of all this I was teaching at Knypersley at the time and my headmaster, Arthur Fryer, was the Chairman.

I have many happy memories including reading for parts under the scrutiny of John Ashton, learning lines, the rehearsals; all great fun. One of the really good things (sometimes disastrous) was painting the scenery beforehand, gathering props, etc. - hopefully ready for the first night. None of these things were chores - we all had a great time, even getting more paint over ourselves sometimes than the backcloth!

I took part in many plays both drama and comedy but my favourite was the latter. The most outstanding memory that I have was playing a maid, a leading role, and an absolutely superb part. During the play Alice Ashton got herself into such a tizzy (as part of the story I must quickly add) and no-one could quieten her down, so, in my capacity as the maid I poured a glass of water out and threw it straight into her face. At rehearsals we both laughed until we cried but when the actual night came it went so perfectly and was so hilarious. She just stood there soaking wet, completely lost for words with gaping mouth, but it literally brought the house down.

Many of my friends preferred to stay offstage - turning their hands to all those things vital to every production, as I'm sure they still are today. Here's to the continuing success of Biddulph Players. I hope present members have as much fun as we all did.

The set for **"To Have and to Hold"**.

The cast and backstage helpers of **"To Have and to Hold"**.
Standing: Rene Stannard, Arthur Gibson, Barbara Copeland, Harry Carthy, Janet Millward, Dorothy Peasegood, Ken Bourne, Harry Machin, Cynthia Brown, Colin Chesterton, Frankie Dean, Sam Reeves, Margaret Goode.
Seated: Megan Porter, Dick Dickinson, Lucy Milne, Peter Averill, Jean Jones, Archie Averill, Frank Galton.

"A Lady Mislaid"
Standing: Betty Lovatt, Hop Hopkinson, Margaret Goode, Len Lee, Sam Reeves, May Hodgkinson.
Seated: Dorothy Peasegood.

OFFICIALS OF BIDDULPH PLAYERS

Chairman ... ... ALFRED T. ROGERS
Hon. Treasurer ... ... HARRY MACHIN
Hon. Secretary ... ... EDWARD A. AVERILL
Stage Manager ... ... PETER AVERILL
Stage Assistants ... ... HARRY MORRIS, JOCK WILSON
Electrician ... ... KENNETH BOURNE
Assistant Electrician... ... ... HARRY CARTHY
Prompters ... ELEANOR AVERILL, MARGARET LIGHTFOOT
Property Mistress ... ... BARBARA COPELAND
Wardrobe Mistress ... ... JANET R. MILLWARD
Scenic Artist ... ... COLIN CHESTERTON
Make-up ... ...TONI MILLER; CYNTHIA BROWN
Business Manager ... ... CYRIL MILLWARD

PRESIDENT - - Lt.-Col. J. W. A. LOVATT

VICE-PRESIDENTS

Mr. S. G. Averill, Mr. S. Dean, Mr. H. Machin, Mr. A. S. Walley, Mr. and Mrs. A. T. Rogers, Mr. C. Millward, Mrs. B. Lovatt, Mr. P. C. Brown, Mr. H. Morris, Miss A. Jones, Miss F. Cottrell, Miss M. J. Cottrell, Mr. W. Stannard, Mr. J. H. Averill, Mr. John Heath, Mr. C. W Moreton, Mr. F. Chaddock, Mr. J. Cottrell, Mr. J. W. Wrigley, Mr. and Mrs. H. Jones, Mr. H. Lees, Mr. D. Machin, Mr. G. L. Kay, Mr. M. F. Rowley, Dr. J. and Mrs. Ferguson, Lt.-Col. W. H. Lees, Miss G. Lees, Mr. S. Lovatt, Mr. W. B. Whitehurst, Mr. J. W. Longman, Mr. S. Quinton, Mr. W. Wingrove

BIDDULPH PLAYERS

THIRD ANNUAL

Dinner Dance

AT THE BIDDULPH ARMS HOTEL

Friday, April 24th, 1953

TICKETS (Members) ——12s. 6d.
(Non-Members) ——15s.

A LADY MISLAID

A COMEDY IN TWO ACTS
— by —
KENNETH HORNE

ACTION OF THE PLAY TAKES PLACE IN THE
NG ROOM AT "MANOR COTTAGE" THE HOME
OF ESTHER AND JENNIFER WILLIAMS

CAST IN ORDER OF APPEARANCE

nall (Daily Woman) ... ... BETTY LOVATT
er (Younger Sister) ... ... MARGARET GOODE
(Elder Sister) ... ... DOROTHY PEASEGOOD
(Detective) ... ... HOP HOPKINSON
... ... SAM REEVES
(Jennifer's Fiance) ... ... LEN LEE
Woman ... ... MAY HODGKINSON

Produced by JOHN ASHTON

T I—SCENE I—EARLY MORNING
SCENE II—THAT EVENING
SCENE III—SOME HOURS LATER
T II—SCENE I—EARLY THE NEXT MORNING
SCENE II—LATER THAT MORNING

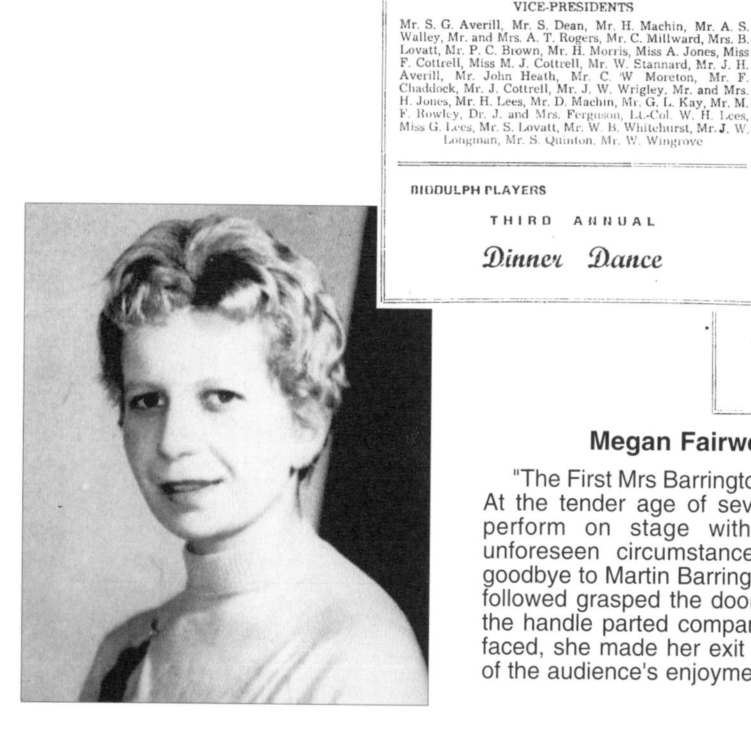

Megan Fairweather(née Porter)

"The First Mrs Barrington" was Megan Porter's first play. At the tender age of seventeen, it is difficult enough to perform on stage without the added challenge of unforeseen circumstances. Megan, after a dramatic goodbye to Martin Barrington, turned, and in the hush that followed grasped the door handle. As it swung open, so the handle parted company with it. Mortified and scarlet faced, she made her exit clutching the handle to the roar of the audience's enjoyment.

The set for **"Arsenic and Old Lace"**.

"Arsenic and Old Lace".
Standing: Sam Knight, Frank Gaulton, Donald Baskeyfield, Arthur Gibson, Margaret Lightfoot, Peter Averill, Ray Colley, Harold Whalley, Donald Smith, Douglas Brown, Roy Davies.
Seated: Doris Page, Cynthia Brown.

"It is probably the best comedy they have staged since their formation. At the opening performance the audience were provided with two and a half hours of almost continuous laughter.

No stranger to Biddulph audiences Peter Averill, who in fact by now has a considerable following, shows how experience helps on stage. Some may criticise because he did not produce an American accent (a nasal accident in a football match prevented it), but his real acting was disclosed in his facial expression. One moment tense, another amorous, Peter Averill did not have to speak at all to `put over' to the audience the state of his mind at a particular stage in the play. A forceful character study, as the dashing young theatre critic Mortimer Brewster."

OFFICIALS OF BIDDULPH PLAYERS

Chairman ... ... ALFRED T. ROGERS
Hon. Treasurer ... ... HARRY MACHIN
Hon. Secretary ... ... EDWARD A. AVERILL
Stage Manager ... ... JOHN ASHTON
Stage Carpenters ... ... JOCK WILSON, ROY DAVIES
Electricians ... ... LEWIS CHADDOCK, HARRY CARTHY
Prompters ... ... JANE LOVATT, MAY HODGEKINSON
Property Mistress ... ... FRANCES M. DEAN
Wardrobe Mistress ... ... JANET R. MILLWARD
Scenic Artist ... ... COLIN CHESTERTON
Make-up ... ... TONI MILLER, CYNTHIA BROWN
Business Manager ... ... CYRIL MILLWARD

PRESIDENT - - Lt.-Col. J. W. A. LOVATT

VICE-PRESIDENTS

Mr. S. G. Averill, Mr. S. Dean, Mr. H. Machin, Mr. A. S. Walley, Mr. and Mrs. A. T. Rogers, Mr. C. Millward, Mrs. B. Lovatt, Mr. P. C. Brown, Mr. H. Morris, Miss A. Jones, Miss F. Cottrell, Miss M. J. Cottrell, Mr. W. Stannard, Mr. J. H. Averill, Mr. John Heath, Mr. C. W. Moreton, Mr. J. Cottrell, Mr. J. W. Wrigley, Mr. and Mrs. H. Jones, Mr. H. Lees, Mr. D. Machin, Mr. G. L. Kay, Mr. M. F. Rowley, Dr. J. and Mrs. Ferguson, Lt.-Col. W. H. Lees, Miss G. Lees, Mr. S. Lovatt, Mr. W. B. Whitehurst, Mr. S. Quinton, Mr. W. Wingrove

NEXT PRODUCTION——

A Play for Ronnie

The Holly and The Ivy

A PLAY IN THREE ACTS

—— by ——

WYNYARD BROWNE

The Play takes place in the Living Room of a Vicarage in Norfolk.

CAST IN ORDER OF APPEARANCE

The Rev. Martin Gregory ... ... Harry Carthy
Jenny (his elder daughter) ... ... Sheila Bower
Margaret (his younger daughter) ... ... May Harvey
Mick (his son) ... ... Sam Knight
Aunt Lydia (his sister-in-law) ... ... Lucy Milnes
Aunt Bridget (his sister) ... ... Eleanor Averill
Richard Wyndham (cousin of his late wife) Bernard James
David Paterson ... ... Alan Harvey

PRODUCED BY DOROTHY PEASEGOOD

SCENES:

ACT I.—Christmas Eve

ACT II.—After dinner the same evening (the curtains are drawn to denote the passage of two hours).

ACT III.—Christmas Morning.

A Comedy by **WARREN CHETHAM STRODE**

April 7th to 10th, 1954

OWING TO UNFORESEEN CIRCUMSTANCES THE PART OF RICHARD WYNDHAM HAS BEEN TAKEN BY PETER AVERILL AT 48 HOURS' NOTICE

A thriller formed within a comedy. It takes place in the house of a doctor in the London suburbs.

"Play for Ronnie"
Standing: Sylvia Peasegood, Peter Averill, Doris Page, Roy Davies, Shirley Adams,
Seated: Megan Porter, Len Lee, Jane Lovatt, Bernard James.

"Will any Gentleman". Standing: Len Lee, Lucy Milnes, Dorothy Pointon, Bernard James, Harold Whalley, Moses Barker, Megan Porter, Roy Davies, Sam Knight.
Seated: May Hodgkinson, Arthur Gibson, Hilda James, Peter Averill.

Henry Stirling has a secret night out and ends up on the stage of a suburban theatre. He succumbs to a hypnotist and returns home still 'under the influence'!

"In the role of Henry Stirling, Arthur Gibson has without doubt produced his best performance yet in a part that keeps him continuously on the stage. He did not fail to provide real comedy entertainment.

"Candied Peel". Standing: Bernard James, Dorothy Pointon, Jean Shaw, Betty Lovatt, Doris Page, Harold Whalley, Fred Dixon. Seated: Hazel Dean, Harry Carthy, Eleanor Averill, Phyllis Lord, Moses Barker.

"Maiden Ladies"
Standing: Hilda James, Don Baskeyfield, Peter Averill, Cynthia Brown, Moses Barker, Bernard James.
Seated: Allan Chambers, Dorothy Pointon, Hazel Dean, Arthur Gibson.

"A distinct feature of recent plays has been the continually improving sets. The scenic decoration this week has been consistent in that it was in keeping with the character of the story. Harry Machin's arrangement of the incidental music was also effective."

The set for "Maiden Ladies".

"As Long as They're Happy"
Standing: Joyce Hancock, Bernard James, Peter Averill, Megan Porter, Allan Chambers, Ronald Hancock.
Seated: Dorothy Pointon, Doris Page, Arthur Gibson, Kathleen Rowley, Len Lee, Phyllis Lord.

Peter Averill

"Husky Peter Averill was well cast as the crooner, who, using an onion to induce tears, adds to his acting efforts snatches of romantic melody."

THE ADVANCEMENT OF MR. SIMPKIN

A Comedy Thriller in Three Acts

BY

JACK LAST

Produced by ——— PETER AVERILL

CAST IN ORDER OF APPEARANCE

HUGH McHUGH	Alan Harvey
MONTGOMERY	Peter Averill
HENRIETTA PHIPPS	Phyllis Lord
BETTY PETERSON	Barbara Hancock
ROSA MIDGELEY	Eleanor Averill
SYBIL FANSHAW-SMITH	Hilda James
MR. SIMPKIN	Don Baskeyfield
MARJORY CRAYSTON	Jean Shaw
SERGEANT BRADFORD	Bernhard James
CHIEF INSPECTOR ROBSON	John Ashton

SYNOPSIS OF SCENES

The action takes place in the office of the Commission for the Prevention of Preventable Diseases

ACT I.

SCENE I.—Time: Morning

SCENE II.—Time: Lunch Time, three months later

ACT II

Next morning

ACT III

The following afternoon

THE PAPER CHAIN

A Drama in Three Acts

BY

FALKLAND L. CARY and IVAN BUTLER

Produced by ——— PETER AVERILL

CAST IN ORDER OF APPEARANCE

ANNE ROBERTS ... Phyllis Lord
JEAN CASSEL ... Dorothy Pointon
MRS. HACKETT ... Lucy Milne
RUBY ... Jean Shaw
JACK HARVEY ... Trevor Lancaster
MRS. DENNISON ... Dorothy Peasegood
MAURICE SPENCER ... Harold Walley
DORIS LAMONT ... Megan Porter
ROBERT NEEDHAM ... Leonard Lee

SYNOPSIS OF SCENES

THE ACTION TAKES PLACE IN THE LOUNGE OF "THE SYCAMORES" HOTEL IN DORSET

ACT I.

SCENE 1—5 p.m. on an April afternoon
SCENE 2—A little before 10.0—same night

ACT II

SCENE 1—A little before noon—next day
SCENE 2—About 3 p.m.—same day

ACT III

SCENE 1—An hour later
SCENE 2—About 8 p.m. that night

BIDDULPH PLAYERS

NEW YEAR'S EVE PARTY

TICKETS — 12s. 6d. (Including Buffet)

Kathleen Thomas (nee Rowley)

John was unaware that Alice, in the part of Mrs. Evans, the duck farmer's wife, intended to go on stage without her false teeth. When she appeared the place was in an uproar.

"Love in a Mist"
Standing: Allan Chambers, Alice Ashton, Peter Averill, Kathleen Rowley
Seated: Joan Basson, Arthur Gibson.

1957 - 58

Barbara Botheras née Unwin

Barbara has been a member since 1955 through the interest her father had with the society. She assisted in preparing the ice-cream which he sold during the interval. At the age of seventeen she joined the cast in “Beside the Seaside”. Forty five years on, having taken on a variety of roles she now enjoys taking a back seat, watching each play four times and selling sweets to our audiences. Her children, Andrew and Louise, have also taken part in many of our plays.

BESIDE THE SEASIDE

A Comedy in Three Acts

BY

LESLIE SANDS

Produced by ——————— JOHN ASHTON

CAST IN ORDER OF APPEARANCE

MRS. AUSTEN (Landlady)	Lucy Milnes
PAT MARLOW	Barbara Botheras
FLORRIE (Maid)	Kathleen Nadin
TONY BRETT	Trevor Lancaster
ETHEL PEARSON	Alice Ashton
WILF PEARSON	Peter Averill
SALLY (Daughter)	Jean Shaw
MR. PEFFER (Honeymoon Couple)	Graham Embury
MRS. PEFFER (Honeymoon Couple)	Margaret Clowes

“Beside the Seaside" was also staged at the Whitehall theatre in London at this time. Mrs Garside, mother of John, had seen both productions and her comment to John Ashton was "you want to go and show them how to do it."

"Lucy Milnes plays the abominable landlady. Alice Ashton's sparkling performance, to everybody's delight she had her eyes blacked. Graham Embrey played his part with endearing stupidity."

A dinner at the Biddulph Arm's Hotel in the 1950s.

The set for “A Lady Mislaid”

The set for “Grand National Night”

Setting the Scene

Ken Machin

I was asked by Peter Averill if I would help out as stage manager, in particular to help to build the set for the Player's production of "Maiden Ladies".

The play was set in the living room of a country house. John Ashton, the producer, outlined what he needed and we were given a plan to show exactly where the window and two doors would have to go. I remember making the doors in my father's workshop, they were in a gothic style with elaborate hinges and covered in studs which I screwed in to add character.

One of the major difficulties was not being able to get into the Gymnasium until the Friday evening, five days prior to the opening night. Before we could start to build the set we had to construct a stage. We started to work at 7 o'clock Friday evening and worked through until the early hours. As many of the helpers went to work on Saturday morning we couldn't start again until after lunch. Quite often it would be 1.00 or 2.00am before we left the Gym. Everything had to be finished for the Tuesday night dress rehearsal, so it was very hard work but we had a lot of willing helpers.

A great deal of the work could be done beforehand and bolted together. We used 3x3 posts either side the platform to hold the proscenium arch and everything was screwed into the floor. This was until the room had a new floor fitted and a way had to be found of securing everything without the use of screws. We had to call upon the ingenuity of Arthur Gibson and Alan Chambers who both worked at `Cowlishaw and Walker'. At work they were able to make special brackets to hold and secure the uprights in position.

The scenery flats were made of sisalcraft, basically a layer of tar sandwiched between two pieces of paper. In those days it was used to put under roofing tiles instead of felt. When new fire regulations came into force they were replaced with jute and fireproofed each time they were used.

With the set completed we hung the heavy velvet brown curtains and installed the winding mechanism to open and close them. The chairs, usually stacked along the sides of the room, were set into rows, usually by the ladies, and more were brought from the Public Hall across the road. Working with Lewis Chaddock, the electrician, I was in charge of everything backstage, and when the opening night arrived my job of stage manager really began!

I made my stage debut in "Sky's the Limit" playing the part of a curate. During rehearsal Arthur Gibson had to hit me over the head with a roll of wallpaper as I perched on the edge of the sofa. Somehow or other his legs became trapped between mine and he fell right over me onto the sofa behind. The producer, Peter Averill, and the rest of the cast laughed so much we kept it in! It was all very nerve racking but great fun.

The set for **"All for Mary"**. Colin Chesterton painted the scenery for this play and many others. He later went on to help out at the Shelton 'Rep' Theatre.

BIDDULPH PLAYERS

PRESENT——

ALL FOR MARY

A FARCE IN THREE ACTS

by HAROLD BROOKE and KAY BANNERMAN

— IN THE —

GYMNASIUM, BIDDULPH

Wed., Thur., Fri., Sat.

MARCH

26th 27th 28th 29th

CAST

ALPHONSE ... Enos Brockley
HUMPHREY MILLAR ... Arthur Gibson
MARY MILLAR ... Margaret Wilkinson
VICTOR MONTENAY ... Alan Chambers
CLIVE NORTON ... George Bell
NANNIE CARTWRIGHT ... Doris Page

TICKETS: Wednesday - 2s.
Thur., Fri., Sat. 2s. 6d. & 3s. 6d.
(All Bookable)

BOOKING PLAN NOW OPEN AT MACHIN'S, OUTFITTERS, HIGH STREET, BIDDULPH. Phone 3196

SUPPORT YOUR LOCAL THEATRE GROUP

"HALF THE CAST NEW TO DRAMA"

"In 'All For Mary' half the cast were making their first appearance in drama. But it would have been hard to tell which they were, for all played their parts in this hotel bedroom farce with verve and confidence.

One of the newcomers was George Bett, who proved to be a master of sarcasm. In the role of Clive Norton, Mary's ex-husband, he finds himself a victim of chicken-pox, together with her present husband, at an hotel in the French Alps, and Mary soon becomes a bone of contention between them.

This was also a first appearance for Enos Brockley, as Alphonse, a member of the hotel staff."

Eddie Cook

Eddie was persuaded to join by Trevor Lancaster in 1959, and appeared as Swindon Scragg in "Till Further Orders". He still remembers the fun everyone had during the rehearsals. In "Wild Goose Chase" he had to run across the stage and throw the goose (actually a duck) back to someone chasing him. Peter Averill was following too close behind and was nearly knocked right off the stage with the force of the heavy bird.

For several plays Eddie was the fire officer and remembers the detailed precautions he had to take. A fire extinguisher had to be close at hand and two bicycle lamps had to be fastened on to the fire escape, one at the top and another at the bottom.

BIDDULPH PLAYERS AMATEUR
DRAMATIC SOCIETY

"Lord Elrood has not quite recovered from his second childhood and lives with an imaginary moat, drawbridge and an enemy spy (the postman).

The set, on a minute stage, was highly convincing of a castle interior room, considering the amount of stage machinery used, all went to show that a firm hand had been at work."

"Wild Goose Chase"
Lucy Milnes, Jean Shaw, David Porter, Trevor Lancaster, Kathleen Rowley, Peter Averill, Harry Hassall, Phyllis Averill, Alice Ashton, Eddie Cook.

"Intent to Murder"
Harry Hassall, Doris Page, Megan Porter, Trevor Lancaster, Harold Whalley, Margaret Clowes.

"As Peter, David Porter (obviously a bright boy) had the difficult task of portraying a dull but sensitive youth, and did it very well. One scene caused great amusement, where he had to caper round the room like an ape, in pursuit of Cissie, charmingly played by Kathleen Nadin."

Fred and brother-in-law Joe come home from the local tavern `laced'. Fred orders sister-in-law Emma (Doris) to dance the seven veils in her nightdress and wallpaper wrappings.

"Sky's the Limit"
Doris Page, Enos Brockley, Alice Ashton, Arthur Gibson, Alan Chambers, Ken Machin, Gervase Barry, Margaret Wilkinson, Kathleen Rowley, David Porter, Peter Averill.

After four weeks of rehearsing one play, John asked the cast what they thought of it. No-one seemed to be very impressed so he changed it to "Till Further Orders". As a result of this change and illnesses, John never had a full cast until the last few days.

"Till Further Orders"
Standing: Doris Page, Trevor Lancaster, Ron Cliffe, Sheila Bennison, Harry Hassall.
Seated: Barbara Botheras, Margaret Clowes, Phyllis Averill, Eddie Cook, Lucy Milnes.

"A triumph for newcomer Pauline Ault. For one whose only previous experience has been in one-act plays put on by Knypersley Youth Club, she gave a remarkably mature performance."

"Dial M for Murder".
Standing: Len Lee, Ron Cliffe. Seated: Trevor Lancaster, Pauline Ault, Peter Averill.

John seems to have been giving his cast a hard time during rehearsals of **"The Feminine Touch"** and Margaret Clowes has obviously had more than enough.

Having first joined the Players at the age of sixteen she appeared in a few of the earlier plays before going to college, rejoining again in 1957.

"The Feminine Touch".

The transformation of a young girl at her uncle's farm, a modern day ugly duckling story.

"In spite of good all-round performances the actress Heather Miller gets most of the credit who in her first appearance at Biddulph played so well the major role of Verity."

"The Feminine Touch"
Standing: Barbara Botheras, Trevor Lancaster, Doris Page, Margaret Clowes, Alice Ashton, Lucy Milnes.
Seated: Heather Miller, Peter Averill, Allan Chambers.

"FOOTBALL COMEDY AT BIDDULPH PLAYERS"

"Biddulph Players' first offering of the season "The Love Match", an exuberant comedy which filled the Gymnasium with merry laughs last week. Lancashire engine driver, Bill Brown is, without doubt, football-crazy. What is more, every time he comes home from a match which his team have lost he is football-mad - usually about the referee."

"The Love Match"
John Whitehurst, Eddie Cook, Doris Page, Betty Davenport, Alice Ashton, Peter Averill, Alan Chambers, Sheila Bennison, Arthur Gibson

"The Secret Tent"
Michael Lightfoot, Dorothy Peasegood, Harry Hassall, Alice Ashton, Trevor Lancaster, Sheila Bennison, Jane Lovatt.

"BRIDE AND THE BACHELOR" 1961

Income			
Sale of tickets	£74	17	6d
Sale of teas	£ 5	13	8d
Sale of programmes	£ 3	5	3d
	£83	16	5d

Expenditure			
Licence		9	0d
Books	£ 4	1	3d
Royalties	£14	0	0d
Property mistress		10	0d
Poster paint		7	6d
A. Birchenhall		9	0d
Box Office expenses		8	6d
Costume hire	£ 4	16	9d
Hire of chairs/room	£ 2	7	6d
Carriage (costume)		6	5d
Printing	£ 9	11	2d
Catering Unionist	£ 3	5	8d
Unionist		5	0d
G Brockley	£ 2	6	11d
Wallpaper etc.	£ 4	0	0d
Unionist Club	£27	15	0d
J.W. Machin	£ 1	17	6d
Haulage		15	0d
	£77	12	2d
Net profit after meeting overheads	£ 6	4	3d

The twenty first production by John Ashton. A farcical comedy. Sir William Bendick Barlow has a mission to complete before entering the pearly gates to settle a bride's nerves.

"The Bride and the Bachelor"
Lucy Milnes, Phyllis Averill, Allan Chambers, Peter Averill, Arthur Gibson, Margaret Wilkinson, Margaret Clowes, Pauline Ault.

"The More the Merrier"
Standing: Sheila Bennison, Lucy Milne, Ron Cliffe, Gervase Barry, Jean Pill, Eddie Cook.
Seated: Pauline Ault, Gillian Knapper, Peter Averill.

Murder Out Of Tune

A PLAY IN THREE ACTS

— BY —

FALKLAND L. CARY

THE ENTIRE ACTION OF THE PLAY TAKES PLACE IN THE LOUNGE OF MICHAEL RENTOR'S FLAT

CAST IN ORDER OF APPEARANCE

SHEILA WARING ... ... Gillian Knapper
MRS. MASON ... ... Jean Pill
LOUIE ... ... Dorothy Peasegood
JACQUELINE CLARKE ... ... Jane Lovatt
MRS. TROCHELL ... ... Alice Ashton
MICHAEL RENTOR ... ... Ronald Cliffe
DR. WARING ... ... Harold Whalley
INSPECTOR HARDING ... ... Trevor Lancaster
MRS. ARNOLD ... ... Minnie Cook

PRODUCED BY PETER AVERILL

ACT I

A SUMMER EVENING ABOUT 10 p.m.

ACT II

THE AFTERNOON OF THE FOLLOWING DAY

ACT III

TWO HOURS LATER

OUR NEXT PRODUCTION WILL BE————

DURING 28th to 31st MARCH, 1962

PROGRAMME

BIDDULPH PLAYERS

JANUARY
1 9 6 2

Murder Out of Tune

FOURPENCE

Jean Pill

Jean joined the society in 1957 and began helping Gladys Brockley with refreshments. The tea was made in the basement of the Gym and the teapots carried through the side door and up the front steps into the hall.

After assisting backstage with props and prompting, she took part in severall plays before taking up front of house duties.

Jean's husband Rob took on the job of business manager, and then over the years various other roles important to the society.

In recognition and appreciation of their dedication to the society, Rob and Jean were made life members in 1999.

"For Pete's Sake"
Standing: Sheila Leyland, Doris Page, Trevor Lancaster, Alice Ashton, Arthur Gibson.
Seated: Ron Lovatt, Jean Pill, Harry Hassall.

"For Pete's Sake"

Pete Mitchell returns to England, having made his fortune in Canada. Millie, who spurned him when he was a youth, hears of his changed fortune and changes her attitude towards him.

"Ron Lovatt played the neighbouring plumber, Charley Perkins, in uproarious fashion, showing not only how to act a drunken scene in professional style, but also the ability to blush when required. Well before the end of the play he had the audience eating out of his hand and raised a laugh each time he walked on stage - a promising debut. Jean Pill gave a splendid portrayal as Doris Perkins the young woman who idolises fast cars and loose pound notes."

"Pool's Paradise"
Harold Walley, Alice Ashton, Harry Hassall, John Whitehurst, Pauline Ault, Lionel Maskery, Sheila Hood.

Sheila Hood

John Ashton knocked on Sheila Hood's door one Sunday morning. He had seen her in a production at Congleton and having been told she lived in Biddulph he wondered if she would consent to be in the Player's next production.

The play was "Pool's Paradise" and Sheila vividly recalls all the laughter at rehearsals with Pauline Ault.

One hilarious moment was when Sheila, as the vicar's wife, discovered him in the cupboard sitting on a stool filling in a football coupon, minus his trousers. After opening the door to reveal all this she had to say the line, "Why are you sitting filling in a pool?" With the action and the pace of the farce, Sheila delivered the line as "Why are you sitting doing a pool?" Having not realised what she had said Sheila wondered why the audience had found it quite so hilarious. Each night after that it was even more impossible to say the line how it should be said.

Although Sheila returned to continue with productions of the operatic society and drama groups in Congleton, a lifelong friendship was formed with Alice and John Ashton.

The Lords' family shop-house is to come down so they barracade themselves in against the authorities. Because of a shortage of actors some were borrowed fron the `Regency Players' at Trentham. It was Trevor Lancaster's first production.

"The Happy Family"
Standing: Lionel Maskery, David Lovatt, Eddie Cook, Michael Lightfoot, Margaret Roberts, Ted Roberts, Sandra Maskery, Helen Wilshaw, Brian Lawton, Seated: Jennifer Brookes, Pamela Whitehurst.

"Love Locked Out"
Margaret Roberts, Ted Roberts, Harry Hassall, Lionel Maskery, Phil Pearce, Helen Wilshaw, Alice Ashton, Pamela Whitehurst.

Betty Davenport
Subscriptions secretary.

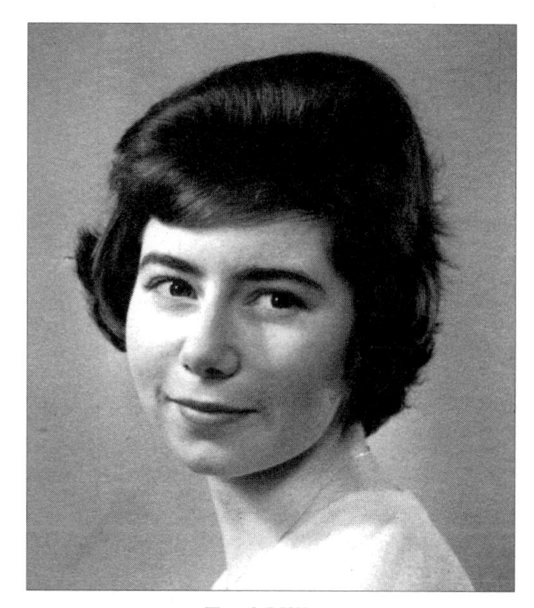

Toni Miller
Make-up.

A Players' dinner dance c. 1962.
Seated centre Colonel Lovatt (President) and Mrs Lovatt.

Early Days at the Gym

Betty Ball (née Davenport)

After the War everyone was anxious to get the country going again. With no cars this meant that many social clubs and societies were set up locally. Biddulph had a 'season', and going to a Player's production was the major event of that season.

I was involved in these productions, more or less from the beginning. My mother used to work in the shop at Knypersley and was approached to become a member when the group was being formed. This she did, along with Mrs Quinn who owned the shop. A short while after this I became a member and started going to rehearsals. I only appeared once on the stage, (one line) as the outraged motorist in "The Love Match".

I did various jobs backstage, prompting, helping Mrs Peasgood with the props, and for a time when Mrs Peasgood was not well, I took on the job of property mistress.

I remember on one of these occasions we needed two wine glasses. I had to go into the Conservative Club next door to the Gymnasium, to try to borrow them. The Club at that time was for "men only", and I was promptly escorted out by a prominent member, and had to wait at the back door. I really felt that I had commited a very serious crime, but that was how it was in those days.

On another occasion, when helping front of house, escorting people to their seats, Mr. Betts, a retired local policeman and caretaker of the Conservative Club, came rushing round to say that a gang of Teddy boys were on their way to Biddulph and would we lock all the doors in case they invaded the premises. Fortunately the crisis did not develop.

I was a member of the social committee which held its meetings at the "Biddulph Arms" or the "Bird in Hand" in Station Road. When I first went I was only in my early twenties and hadn't told my father where I was going, and by the time I arrived home he knew I had been spotted entering a public house!

On the social side I attended most of the dances, parties, visits to the theatre and to the seaside. I remember going on a trip to Morecambe and it was such a wet day we persuaded the driver to take us to Blackpool to see the lights. As we were moving slowly through the lights some of the men from 'Costains' started fooling about with water pistols, jumping off the coach and refilling them with the rainwater from puddles in the gutter. As you can imagine everyone had seen quite enough rainwater for one day, tempers flared and the water pistols were confiscated.

When Peter and Phyllis Averill were leaving the district we arranged a leaving party for them. When the evening arrived, everyone had gathered at the Biddulph Arm's except the two guests of honour. It appeared no-one had told them! When someone went to fetch them Peter was working in the garden and Phyllis was on a school trip to London. Peter had a quick change and joined us at the party!

For a number of years I was subscription secretary and worked closely with Lucy Milnes the treasurer. I relinquished that job in 1970 when my father was seriously ill. After his death, I returned for a further five years.

Plays performed in The Gymnasium

	TITLE	AUTHOR	PRODUCER
1949/50	"Wishing Well"	Eynon Evans	John Ashton
1950/51	" Young Mrs. Barrington"	Warren Strode	John Ashton
	"Grand National Night"	D. & C. Christie	Harry D. Lees
	"The Blue Goose"	Peter Blakemore	Fred Dixon
	"When We Are Married"	J. B. Priestley	John Ashton
1951/52	"Heaven & Charing Cross"	Aubrey Danvers-Walker	John Ashton
	"Without the Prince"	Philip King	John Ashton
	"The Paragon"	R. & M. Pertwee	John Ashton
1952/53	"The Good Young Man"	Kenneth Horne	John Ashton
	"To Have and to Hold"	Lionel Brown	Dorothy Peasegood
	"A Lady Mislaid"	Kenneth Horne	John Ashton
1953/54	"Arsenic and Old Lace"	Joseph Kesselring	John Ashton
	"The Holly and the Ivy"	Wynyard Browne	Dorothy Peasegood
	"Play for Ronnie"	Warren Chetham-Strode	Dorothy Peasegood
1954/55	"Will Any Gentleman"	Vernon Sylvaine	John Ashton
	"Candied Peel"	Fawkland L. Cary	Peter Averill
	Maiden Ladies"	Guy Paxton	John Ashton
1955/56	"As Long as They're Happy"	Vernon Sylvaine	John Ashton
	"The Advancement of Mr Simpson"	Jack Last	Peter Averill
1956/57	"The Paper Chain"	Fawkland L. Cary	Peter Averill
	"Love in a Mist"	Kenneth Horne	John Ashton
1957/58	"Beside the Seaside"	Leslie Sands	John Ashton
	"All for Mary"	Harold Brooke/K. Bannerman	Peter Averill
1958/59	"Wild Goose Chase"	Derek Benfield	John Ashton
	"Intent to Murder"	Leslie Sands	Peter Averill
	"Sky's the Limit"	Arnold Helsby	John Ashton
1959/60	"Till Further Orders"	Wilfred Massey	John Ashton
	"Dial M for Murder"	Frederick Knott	John Ashton
	"The Feminine Touch"	Wilfred Massey	John Ashton
1960/61	"The Love Match"	Glen Melvyn	John Ashton
	"The Bride & the Bachelor"	Ronald Millar	John Ashton
	"The Secret Tent"	Elizabeth Addyman	Peter Averill
1961/62	"The More the Merrier"	Ronald Millar	John Ashton
	"Murder Out of Tune"	Fawkland L. Cary	Peter Averill
	"For Pete's Sake"	Leslie Sands	John Ashton
1962/63	"Pool's Paradise"	Philip King	John Ashton
	"The Happy Family"	Michael C. Hutton	Trevor Lancaster
	"Love Locked Out"	David Kirk	John Ashton

A POTTED HISTORY
PART II: 1963-1971 BATEMAN GIRL'S SCHOOL
Doris Page

We left the Gymnasium in 1963 and moved to Bateman School (now Park Middle). This was at the time that the Town Hall was being built and the Gymnasium was needed to temporarily house the council office staff.

It was a very difficult time for the Society with a new venue and the loss of some of the original members. However, it was a real joy to perform on the school stage. It meant no more handling of that proscenium arch or heavy velvet curtains. There was lots of room both sides of the stage. It was very good from the Players point of view, but even if we had a hundred people in the audience, they were completely lost in such a big hall.

The first play we staged at Bateman School was called "The Happiest Days of Your life" and was produced by John Ashton. The huge stage had to be draped with curtaining, as a temporary measure while the flats were being altered and extended. In the interval the audience were able to move to another room for refreshments, supplied by Eileen Ellerton.

Our second play there was "Wanted One Body" and we decided to write to the local schools to invite the schoolchildren to attend the Tuesday performance. The charge was 1/6 per child and we had a very good response. The hall was almost full and the little dears cheered like mad when I was knifed in the back! A happy and very noisy evening was enjoyed by all. However for some reason the idea was dropped, I don't remember it happening again.

My husband, Harry Page, became a member at this time and acted as stage manager and set designer. He came as a direct result of a game of billiards with Phil Pearce. He remained in this capacity for about twenty years until Ken Tunstall took over, and he still comes along to every play to help build the sets.

I remember one Friday night when we were doing a play, the heavens opened at about 7.00pm and the rain was torrential. This was just the time when people were setting out for the performance and consequently we ended up with only three people in the audience. I remember it was Dorrie Machin and her two sons Garth and Neville. They hardly missed a play; so we played to the three of them!

Miss Weller, the Head Teacher, made us very welcome and all went well for a time. We did have a few dramas though, behind the scenes. On one occasion we were in a panic over the non-arrival of our costumes from Manchester for "Ladies in Retirement". They were eventually discovered sitting on Congleton station, addressed simply "Biddulph". Trevor Lancaster, the producer, collected them on the opening night. We had not seen them before, but luckily they all fitted perfectly.

Another time, I was taking the lead in "House on the Cliff" and became ill with pneumonia. On the Monday we considered cancelling the play but the rest of the cast were keen to carry on, and they talked Pauline McLellan into taking on the part (she had been prompting). It happened to be half-term and as she was a teacher, she was on holiday, She worked very hard to learn the part, which was quite a big one, so quickly. The Wednesday performance was cancelled, although a few people turned up and were allowed to stay. Pauline went on on the Thursday without a book and she was brilliant.

In November 1968 I produced my first play. I remember it was a real problem choosing a play, due to the shortage of male members at the time. I eventually settled for "Ladykiller" with a female cast of nine. It was the first time that we had an all female cast. We had the same problem when we tried to cast the next play,. "What's Hatching". However we were fortunate to be able to borrow three actors from Kidsgrove Dramatic Society

When the headmistress Miss Weller left ,she was replaced by Miss Hey who did not like the school being used in the evenings other than for school activities. Consequently after nearly eight years, we were once again having to find a new venue.

1963 - 64

"CHANGE OF VENUE A SUCCESS"

"Less work and more pleasant atmosphere for Biddulph Players. 'The Happiest days of your Life' was one of those farces which strain the capacities of audience and actors as well, and the evening was saved only by the talents of the leading players, who turned superficial and not very original characters into people in which it was easy to believe."

Helen Wilshaw, who appeared as one of the parents in the play remembers hearing the news of the death of President Kennedy while they were rehearsing.

"The Happiest Days of Your Life"
Standing: Margaret Roberts, Helen Wilshaw, Trevor Lancaster, Betty Hall, Alice Ashton, Harold Whalley, Phil Pearce, Lucy Milnes, Eddie Cook.
Seated: Harry Hassall, Ted Roberts, Stephen Lloyd, Priscilla Harris.

"The hour is come but not the man"

Harry Page

I had been associated with Biddulph Players since 1950 but it wasn't until 1963 that I began to take a more active role. A certain chairman of the Players arrived at my door, looking extremely panic-stricken, asking for help. It appeared they had started to rehearse a play and had no-one for backstage manager. He said it did not involve much work and in any case there were plenty of assistants available, so I agreed to help out.

The following evening I went along to the school hall, where the rehearsals were being held. I remember sitting and watching a half a dozen people with books, moving backwards and forwards across an open stage with a man at the front shouting instructions to move from one position to another.

After about an hour someone shouted "tea" and everyone on the stage disappeared. I saw my opportunity to have a few words with the man in charge, Mr John Ashton. He asked if he could see me nearer to the time when the play was due to go on.

A few weeks later I walked into the hall and found the same people on the stage, some with books and some without. John Ashton seemed very displeased and at one point dropped his head in his hands and muttered something about "God!" Thankfully the tea arrived at this point and relieved the situation.

I asked John why the leading lady always fell flat on her face whenever she reached a certain point on the stage. He replied that that was where the bookcase would be, and as I had brought the subject up, could I make one about 6' 6". He also wanted some castors on it so that it could be pushed.

On further reflection I realised that a full case of books would be heavy to push so I painted some pieces of card to look like books. I assured myself that no-one in the hall, certainly at the back, would notice. To ensure that it would run in the right direction I nailed wooden slats to the floor and put a stop on the end to prevent it careering around the stage .

On the Saturday morning before the week of the play the flats and the scenery were delivered. After an hour or two of hammering, bracing and clamping, we had the semblance of a three-walled room, complete with bookcase. When it was finished I asked John who was going to push the bookcase on. He explained that the lady who had been falling flat on her face had been stabbed in the back by a man coming from out of the bookcase. This man would move it. My job now involved the lights, curtains, sound effects and seeing that everyone was on stage when they were supposed to be. John told me not to worry!

Tuesday arrived, the day of the dress rehearsal. The leading lady gave a very good performance of being stabbed in the back, despite the non-appearance of the man in the bookcase. John was pleased and said it would be alright on the night.

When the play opened there was great excitement and a pleasant anticipatory hum in the hall. All was ready for the first of my sequences, the lights. Then John rushed in with a knife and a blackout curtain. The bookcase man had not turned up and I would have to take his place! Shrouded in black I think I gave a reasonable stabbing performance, because, peeping through the curtain later, a man on the front row gave me the "thumbs up" sign. All in all my debut on stage, thankfully passed unnoticed.

"Wanted One Body". Standing: Trevor Lancaster, Arnold Williams, Barbara Howells, Harold Whalley, Pauline Ault, Eddie Cook. Seated: Doris Page, Melva Copeland, Cliff Ellerton.

"A Victorian thriller in which housekeeper strangles mistress of the house"

"Pick of the acting was that of Alice Ashton, who never faltered in her difficult role as the housekeeper and Lionel Maskery as her nephew who provided sketches of humour to the otherwise serious play. Making their first appearance with the Players, Anne Pearce, Gladys Williams and Hazel Brereton showing themselves to be welcome additions."

"Ladies in Retirement"
Standing: John Heath, Gerald Wade, Harry Page, Cliff Ellerton, Barbara Howells, Christine Sherratt, Phil Pearce, Eileen Ellerton, Harry Morris, Doris Page, Anne Pearce, Sylvia Johnson, Arnold Williams, Pauline Ault, Trevor Lancaster, Betty Davenport.
Seated: Lucy Milnes, Hazel Brereton, Alice Ashton, Gladys Williams, Lionel Maskery.

Harry Hassall

"APPENDIX ALMOST COST HIM HIS PART"

Biddulph Players almost had to go ahead with their latest production last Wednesday without one of the main characters, Harry Hassall, who was rushed to the City General on Tuesday with suspected appendicitis.

In desperation they called in Cyril Bennett, of Kidsgrove Players, to take the part, which he knew through having played it at Kidsgrove. But only hours before the Wednesday performance, Harry returned from hospital to take his part and Cyril stood by during the performance just in case Harry had to be rushed back.

Watching Harry taking the part of Albert Grimshaw one would never have suspected that he had just come from hospital. He put his ailment at the back of his mind and gave an impeccable performance."

Arnold William's first production. A Lancashire comedy involving two Russian engineers who come to stay with the Grimshaws to study English life.

"Friends and Neighbours"
Standing: Cyril Bennett, Barbara Botheras, Cliff Ellerton, Hazel Brereton, Trevor Lancaster, Gerald Wade,
Seated: Doris Page, Barbara Howells.

"Flat Spin"
Standing:
Trevor Lancaster, Barbara Howells, Alice Ashton.
Seated:
Hazel Brereton, Cliff Ellerton.

"A Murder Has Been Arranged"
Standing: Malcolm Haydon, Lucy Milnes, Doris Page, Anne Pearce, Tony Mayer, Arnold Williams, Gladys Williams.
Seated: Pauline Ault, Harry Hassall.

"A MURDER WENT AHEAD AS PLANNED"

"The one defect in Trevor Lancaster's production is that the characters hardly ever seem to be surprised by anything when they should be scared out of their wits. The poisoner of the piece is played by Harry Hassall with the languid attitude universally adopted by stage journalists, but he gives the character plenty of dry humour in a performance which holds the play together. His victim, poisoned for money, played by Arnold Williams, dies harrowingly after the wholly predictable moment when the drinks are switched. It was a wonder that the players were not on edge, for the costumes arrived from Manchester only half an hour before the curtain rose. If they had not come, the producer was all ready for a very different murder to be arranged"

"'Send up' of a Lancashire boarding house holiday"
"The steamroller personality of landlady Mrs Austin was played with enthusiasm and confidence by Gladys Hall. This was her first `dabble' in amateur theatricals and she played the role with a fiery determination."

"Beside the Seaside"
Standing: Gladys Hall, Tony Mayer, Margaret Parkinson, Malcolm Haydon, Hazel Brereton, Trevor Lancaster, Sheila Hood. Seated: Alice Ashton, Barbara Howells.

Margaret Fernyhough (nee Parkinson)

Initially persuaded by Hazel Brereton to go along for the production of `Beside the Seaside', Margaret found herself cast as the Pearson's daughter Sally. She was amused and fascinated watching Alice Ashton every night at rehearsal having a glass of water thrown into her face. By opening night the timing was perfect - and the audience loved it.

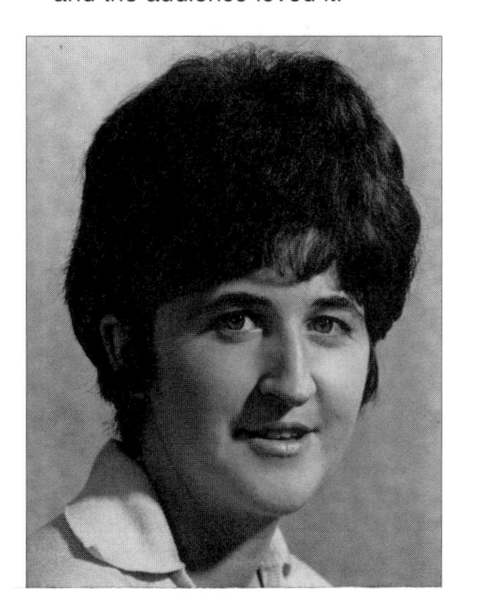

Gladys Williams

Gladys was in drama productions from the age of 5 and she joined the Players with her husband Arnold in 1964. Through the Bateman years she helped with make-up and she has assisted with front of house with every play since she joined. When Arnold was 80, the society made them both life members.

"An actor's life for me"

Arnold Williams Remembered

Doris worked at the school where Arnold's wife Gladys was a teacher. She had told her they were having casting problems with the society's second play at Bateman and wondered if Arnold would be interested, and he agreed to take on the part of Mr Blundell in "Wanted One Body" at the eleventh hour. He remained with the society for the next 34 years!

Arnold had first trodden the boards as a boy scout. When he was 17 he joined the student's theatre in Leeds performing with many actors who later became famous on stage and screen. The celebrated Peter O'Toole shared the same role as Arnold in one particular pantomine, playing it on alternate weeks. During this period there were many drama groups in the city of Leeds and the actors moved between those groups. Arnold gained a wealth of experience and became a man of many parts. It even included some professional walk on parts when he actually got paid for his work.

One day on stage in Leeds he stood at the bottom of a great staircase waiting for his stage wife to appear. After what seemed to be an eternity of waiting he made the decision to leave the stage and go in search of his lost wife. He discovered her locked in the ladies toilet unable to get out!

Arnold's father was senior area sales manager at Cadburys so at the age of seventeen Arnold joined the firm and went to work in the office. It was there that he first met the 16 year old office girl who was to become his wife. War broke out and Arnold went into the forces where he met a headmaster who was to change his life - suggesting that he might enjoy a career in teaching, so when the War was over he took his advice, left Cadburys and went to college. When he qualified he came to Biddulph where he took up an appointment at Bateman School where he taught until his retirement in 1971.

In 1985, with another teacher, Harry Hassall, and other friends in Biddulph Players, the children's theatre was set up. Based at Bateman School it was to entertain the children of Biddulph and the surrounding area for the next ten years, putting on plays such as "Wizard of Oz", "Owl and the Pussycat" and "Snow White".

Arnold's most memorable roles in the Players were those of Henry Hobson in "Hobson's Choice" and the upright father in "Spring and Port Wine". Acting in "Tomb with A View" as the family solicitor, he had to read out the will. He found the contents of the piece of paper handed to him very interesting. So much so that there was dead silence for quite some time with the audience waiting in anticipation and Arnold completely engrossed, quite oblivious of prompts.

Drama was the main passion of his life, his one and only interest. He remained a member of the society until his death in 1998. During that time he played many parts and produced many plays. He was President of the society from 1982 to 1995 and in 1991 he was made a life member. He was a dedicated and supportive member.

Arnold Williams

'Childrens Theatre' production of **"Wizard of Oz"**.

'Childrens Theatre' production of **"Snow White and the Seven Dwarfs"**.

"The Sound of Murder"
Standing: Cliff Ellerton, Hazel Brereton, Harold Whalley.
Seated: Arnold Williams, Margaret Parkinson, Tony Mayer.

Cliff Ellerton

Cliff came to help backstage and the inevitable happened, he was cast in a play straight away.

He appeared in several plays at Bateman and his wife Eileen assisted with the teas and front of house duties. He was also a member of Kidsgrove Players.

Harold Whalley

Malcolm Haydon was listed in the programme as the Inspector, but due to a bereavement he did not appear. His part was taken over by Harold Whalley reading his lines from the book.

Pre-nuptial complications for Geoffrey Cooper, commercial artist.

"The play was the funniest seen in Biddulph for some time and the applause and laughs the players received from an appreciative audience were fully deserved"

"Double Trouble"
Mary Moss, Michael Lightfoot, Annette Vallerley, Malcolm Haydon, Hazel Brereton, Harry Hassall.
Seated: Doris Page, Barbara Howells, Trevor Lancaster, Sheila Leyland.

Mary Moss

As a chuntering landlady, Mary was dismayed to find the vacuum cleaner disintegrating in the middle of the opening scene. It called for some professional ad-libing and the audience responded by clapping enthusiastically.
John Ashton admitted to starting the applause off, so much did he appreciate the unrehearsed moment.

Hazel Brereton

Hazel Brereton's first stage appearance was in "Ladies in Retirement". On stage with Doris she realised how good it was to be with an experienced professional. During one performance Hazel was at a complete loss to remember her next line (one thing we all dread). Doris sensed it immediately, probably by the look on her face, and jumped in to save the day.
"Double Trouble" was a favourite play of Hazel's especially one particular line - "ee, I do like your hat." The review of this play commented on her portrayal of Mrs. Sawyer as the "Performance of a lifetime."

1967 - 68

"Cat Among the Pigeons"
Standing: Mike Adams, Philip Austin, Cliff Ellerton, Doris Page.
Seated: Pauline McLellan, Margaret Parkinson, Trevor Lancaster, Alice Ashton, Susan Bailey.

Soldier son returns from Far East with fan dancer.

"Undoubtedly the star of the play was Grandma, admirably impersonated by Alice Ashton. The wittiest of the characters, her sparkling humour had the audience rolling in their seats."

"House on the Cliff"
Standing: Malcolm Haydon, Mike Adams, Hazel Brereton, Pauline McLellan.
Seated: Trevor Lancaster, Annette Valleley, Sheila Leyland.

Cliffhanger

Pauline McLellan

Half term. A week of no early risings, no jostling for position on the busy A34. In short, a week of doing nothing. And then the telephone rang and the pursuit of idleness just slipped away. It was Trevor Lancaster, producer of `House on the Cliff' and one of the leading ladies had fallen ill. Could I step in at short notice? When was the play to go on? Well, the first night is tomorrow, but we'll cancel the first night. You needn't learn the part. Just walk on with the book. Er, do you have a tape recorder? It could be helpful in learning the lines.

A few hours later the borrowed tape recorder arrived and I set forth to learn the part of Karen. I had never learned my lines as such before. I had always found that when the producer said that at the next rehearsal there would be no books somehow or other the lines came out of my head. Well, more or less.

"House on the Cliff' went before an audience at the Bateman Girls' school a day late. I remember nothing of the plot now; perhaps I never did know what the play was about; but no script was used on stage and only one small prompt during the remainder of the run. Phew!

Pauline McLellan (nee Ault)

"THE GIRL WITH THE FURROWED BROW SOLVES PLAYERS' PROBLEM"

"Only the pluck of one of the members and the courage of the producer enabled Biddulph Players to raise the curtain for their latest production "House on the Cliff" last night. When one of the leading ladies Doris Page was taken ill this week producer Trevor Lancaster was all set to call the whole thing off until prompter Pauline McLellan started learning Doris's important part."

THE GIRL WITH A FURROWED BROW

Pauline McIntyre looks just as she feels—worried to death as she makes a start on memorising her lines! Helping her is Mike Adams. (Chronicle photo 232/68)

Solves Players' problem

"Blithe Spirit"
Standing: Millicent Hurst, Melva Williams, Annette Vallerley,
Seated: Margaret Parkinson, Trevor Lancaster, Gladys Hall, Harry Hassall.

"Eternal triangle involving the ghost of first wife"

"Melva Williams gave a superb performance as the wife of Charles. She made the production come to life and the audience squirm under her endless arguments with hubby. It felt as though one had accidently walked in when the neighbours were arguing."

Gladys Hall

Gladys made her debut as the landlady in "Beside the Seaside" complete with hairnet and curlers. Her second role was the clairvoyant, Madame Arcati, in Noel Coward's "Blithe Spirit", a role made famous by Margaret Rutherford. This was a very demanding role which necessitated Harry Page to administer a 'wee medicinal dram' between scenes.

Many Selectus employees filled the hall to give moral support to their colleague Gladys. During the séance scene when Madame Arcati says in hushed tones those famous lines, "Is there anybody there?" a voice from the back called out, "Yes me, your little fat friend!"

"All's Well That Ends Well"

Malcolm Haydon

I joined the Biddulph Players in 1960, recruited by Derek Rogers, a neighbour of mine who was the stage electrican. I took the part of Cavendish in "A Murder has been Arranged".

Someone had told me that John Ashton had a very short fuse and was difficult to work with. I found this to be completely untrue. He knew what he wanted and got it. He chose plays he knew our audience would enjoy. I remember during one rehearsal, he stopped the action and said, "When this play goes on, you will look the fools if you don't know your lines and not me." It was said quietly but had the desired effect; the play improved enormously from then on.

The funniest moment I can recall was when acting with Alan Hart and we had to carry quite a portly lady across the stage and put her on the settee. No easy task especially when Alan under his breath muttered "Never mind the quality, feel the width." The remark so amused me that I just burst out laughing and we nearly dropped the lady on the floor.

Another hilarious moment was when Alan actually fell asleep when the curtains closed. He had been playing one of the guests at an old people's home and because of lack of space on stage we had put him in front of the curtain. His only part was to hobble on and to feign sleep - but he did it too well!

One of the most hilarious plays in which I took a part was "Dangerous Corner". I must add that it was not meant to be. It was, in fact, a tragic drama, one of J B. Priestley's time plays. The cast included two players borrowed from Kidsgrove Drama Society, normally much happier with comic parts. The overall performance was so bad that we reduced the play to a farce. One member of the cast had to be permanently seated by a hole in the scenery wall with his own personal prompter on the other side feeding him every line. The review in the paper particularly mentioned his relaxed performance,

I produced my first play "Love in a Mist" shortly after moving to Knypersley First School, but gained most satisfaction producing the plays of Alan Acykbourn, especially "Time and Time Again". My proudest moment was when I received the "Irene Gartside Memorial Trophy' for my production of this play.

"Members of Biddulph Players took a night off on New Year's Eve and held a successful party at the Biddulph Arms." M.C. was Mr H. Bailey and delicious refreshments were served by Mrs Moses. Seated: H Page (stage manager) D Page (social secretary) Mr A Wilshaw (President), Mrs Wilshaw, Mr H Morris (secretary), J Alcock.

"Who-dun-it with an all-female cast"

"The first play produced by Doris Page. She explained: `We are desperately short of male acting members and that is why we have had to do this play. This is the first time we have had an all-female cast and we hope it will be the last'."

"Lady Killer"
Annette Valleley, Jennifer Alcock, Moira Potts, Doris Page (director), Sheila Leyland, Jean Donn, Susan Bailey. Seated: Millicent Hurst, Hazel Brereton, Margaret Parkinson.

"Bouquets for best acting went to Alice Ashton as the nosey neighbour, Mrs Fox, and Pauline McLellan, as the rather sophisticated man-hunter, Lily White. Their performances were faultless and they carried off their characterisations very convincingly."

"What's Hatching"
Standing: Eric Birch, Pat Hood, Pauline McLellan, Michael Lightfoot, Reg Dunbill, Cyril Bennett.
Seated: Alice Ashton, Melva Williams, Doris Page, Moira Potts.

"Stolen business cheque, accidental death and love revelations"

"The problem of a shortage of men in the society has recently been overcome with the appearance last week of Reg Dunbill, Malcolm Haydon and Eric Birch."

"Dangerous Corner"
Standing: Reg Dunbill, Eric Birch, Millicent Hurst, Hazel Brereton, Annette Valleley. Seated: Malcolm Haydon, Moira Potts.

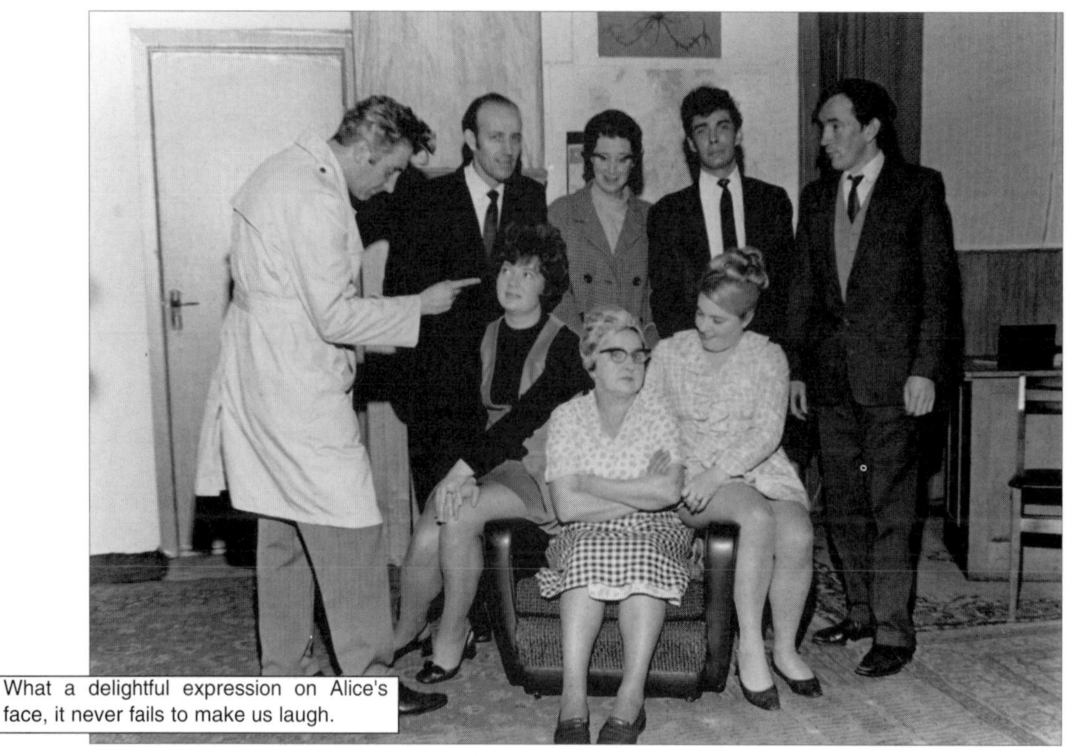

What a delightful expression on Alice's face, it never fails to make us laugh.

"Busybody"
Standing: Trevor Lancaster, Cyril Bennett, Doris Page, Tony Goldstraw, Frank Gilmartin.
Seated: Pat Hood, Alice Ashton, Pat Gilman.

Two families book their annual holiday together in a rented house. From the word go, things go wrong.

"Sheila Leyland, who plays Natalie Sparling, was called upon to do the part at almost a moments notice, for the original actress was a victim of the `flu'. She carried the part along with confidence, and her lack of rehearsal was undetected."

"This Happy Home"
Standing: Sylvia Gibson, Cyril Bennett, Pauline Ault, Tony Goldstraw.
Seated: Malcolm Haydon, Melva Williams, Sheila Leyland.

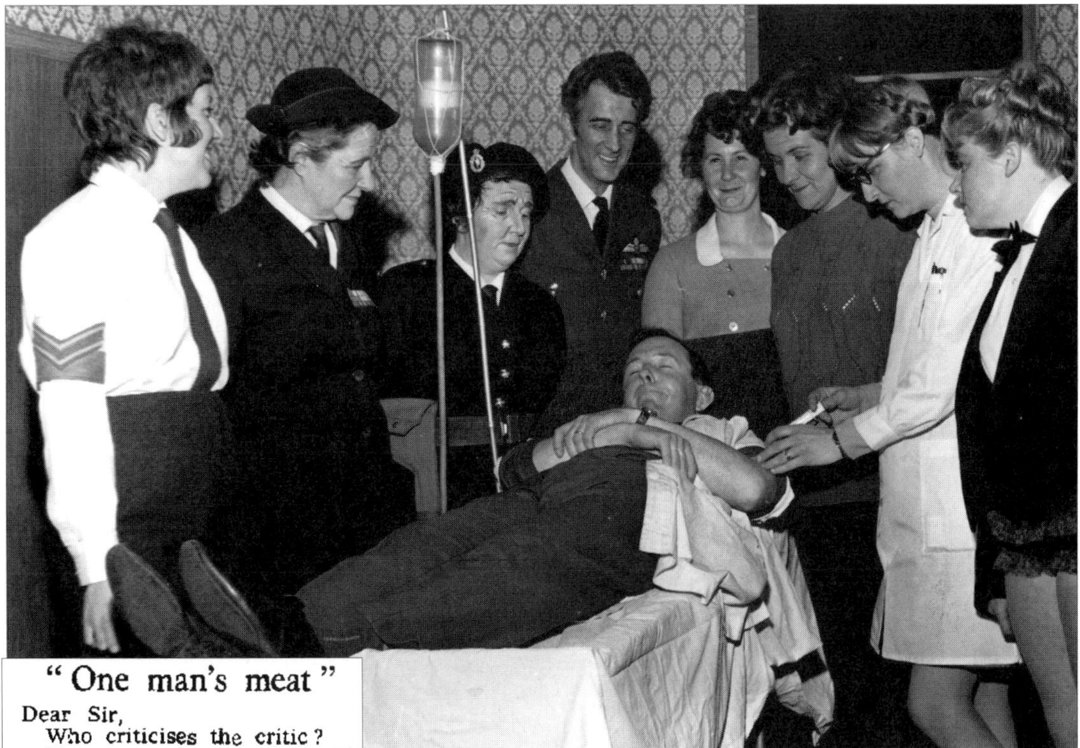

"No Time for Figleaves"
Melva Williams, Gladys Williams, Sylvia Gibson, Trevor Lancaster, Annette Valleley, Hazel Brereton, Sheila Leyland, Pat Gilman.
Reclining: Malcolm Haydon.

"One man's meat"

Dear Sir,

Who criticises the critic?

Here is a classic point with regard to your man's report on the Biddulph Players' production of "No time for fig leaves" this week.

This report was, in my opinion and that of all the people who saw and enjoyed this play, a monstrous misrepresentation of this performance.

The audience obviously enjoyed this amusing comedy, and there were one or two outstanding performances. Trevor Lancaster and Melva Williams were particularly good and the play as a whole moved slickly and was fine entertainment.

Your critic's review was mediocre in style, in content, and in realism.—Yours si

Trevor Lancaster

Trevor appeared regularly in the lead roles from his first appearance at the Gym in 1956 until he left the society in 1970 shortly after his marriage.

The heart-throb of many ladies in the audience, he had a large following of fans. After reading a very scathing report in the Chronicle many of them wrote to the editor and to the critic personally. The critic was inundated with letters, so much so that he wrote a letter of complaint to the society requesting them to try to put a stop to them.

Dear Sir,

Who is the poor man's Bernard Levin you have working for you as a so-called critic? I find it difficult to believe that he saw the same production as we did last week (Biddulph Players' production of "No time for fig leaves").

The play was most amusing and enjoyable and for the audience as a whole there was never a dull moment. The acting, especially by Trevor Lancaster, Melva Williams and Pat Gilman, was of an excellent standard, and to not even give these players a mention borders on criminal.

In conclusion, I would suggest that your "critic" keeps his ulcerated, distorted comments to himself, where they truly belong, for his unenlightened opinion is his and his alone. — Yours sincerely,

Clashes of a family with their domineering father, a Lancashire working man, as he struggles to retain authority .

"Possibly the most striking performance was that of Wilfred Crompton, played by Julian Hirst. Fifteen year old Julian, still a pupil of Knypersley Hall School, gave an extremely good performance, being sure of his lines and confident."

"Spring and Port Wine"
Standing: Valerie Mellenchip, Doris Sabberwal, Michael Lightfoot, Alan Hart, Sylvia Gibson.
Seated: Alice Ashton, Julian Hirst, Arnold Williams.

"Queen's birthday honours, infidelity and much marital mix-up"

"The six strong cast really let rip with Paul Jones' bright comedy of marital stresses, and there were some outstanding performances. Perhaps the most notable of these came from Doris Sabberwal, as the unbelievable tweedy Beatrice, who looked all the time as though she would have been more at home in a stable than a wealthy London residence. She proved herself to be an actress of considerable ability, with her delightful swaggering walk and spinsterish cardigans."

"Birthday Honours"
Standing: Sylvia Gibson, Elizabeth Holland, Melva Williams.
Seated: John Gilman, Doris Sabberwal, Malcolm Haydon

"New Year's Eve was a double celebration for members of Biddulph Players. In addition to seeing in the New Year in 1971, they also marked the fact that it was twenty-one years since the society was formed. The President John Ashton is seen cutting the cake, made by Mr S A Bowcock, to mark the anniversary."

"Brief Suspicion"
Standing: Doris Page, Annette Valleley, Sheila Leyland, Pauline McLellan.
Seated: Alice Ashton, Hazel Brereton.

"Murder who-dun-it"

"Of the seven players, Hazel Brereton, who played the solicitor was the most outstanding, and despite the fact that she had been ill during some rehearsal time, she was sure of her lines and put a great deal of expression into her acting and stage manner."

Storage, Trials and Tribulations

Harry Page

As an addendum to our history we thought we should acknowledge the heavers of wood, drawers of water and knockers-in of nails who over the last half-century have assisted in the not-so glamorous, but equally satisfying, side of amateur dramatics. These include the transporters, builders and general handlers of stage paraphernalia, without whom it would be difficult for amateur dramatics to exist.

In the beginning of the society some of the stage furniture was made privately but much else, furniture, flats, etc., were constructed in very difficult circumstances in a back room of the 'Bird in Hand' public house in Station Road. It says much for the sobriety of our joiners/carpenters, with so much liquid sustenance at hand, that items were so expertly constructed. Some of the original items are still in use, some with various adaptations. In fact, the original flats have only now received their 50th-year facelift. They were stripped and recovered and fifty years of dried paste with fifty years of wallpaper design were mercifully disposed of. They had become excessively heavy!

Storage of our property was either at the gymnasium or in the room to the rear of the 'Bird in Hand' until about 1964. About that time the two cottages and prefabs which had housed the council were being demolished. The building of the new town hall had begun and the council staff took over the gymnasium for use as offices. The Players, who by this time had amassed a great deal of property, were then deprived of it. A store was urgently required.

After many enquiries, and following up many suggestions, we were fortunate in being offered the use of a vacant room over a garage and outbuildings in a property which backed on to Albert Street. The room itself, which had been a workshop, was ideal. However, access from the yard was via a narrow wooden stairway and not suitable for the manhandling of bulky items. Undeterred and with their stage-building techniques (and taking a tip from men of old whose stretcher-bound friends wished to get close to Jesus but could not do so because of the crush) they decided on the hole in the roof method. A door was inserted high up in the wall of the workshop and the problem was solved. Loading and unloading was then effected from the back of a lorry parked on the pavement below the door. So, if those who take their leisurely Sunday afternoon's stroll down Albert Street are curious as to the reason why a door should be set in a wall so high above road level, there is the answer.

The door in the workshop end wall in Albert Street giving the Players access to their props.

From 1964 to about 1972 we occupied the aforementioned premises under two different owners, for which we were extremely grateful. Developments there, however, meant that we had to transfer our stage stock to another place. Another place was the very roomy garage of one of our members. This deprived his car of very comfortable lodgings for a season or so, but it was very unsatisfactory considering the amount and range of equipment we had to store.

In 1973/74 the Players, feeling they could no longer impinge upon our member's good offices, sought around for another storeroom. Desperation followed. But then providence really did come to our assistance. It arrived in the help of the Church at Biddulph Moor. We were given permission to store larger parts of stage items in the old church school in Church Lane. The smaller items were packed into the outside toilet block in the school yard. This block is of the 19th century variety and does not have lighting. Loading and unloading there on a dark, wet, gale-blowing night was never the best way of spending an evening. Inevitably, ferreting around in the dark for certain articles required for the stage produced exclamations of "Oh dear!" or some such oath (in deference to being on church property) by those engaged in the operation.

Permission to store at the school had come at a time when it seemed we had exhausted all possible alternatives. So it was a move for which we shall always be grateful. From Biddulph Moor we transported the stores, scenery, etc to Park Middle School where the plays had been performed. And when in 1971 when we transferred to Knypersley First School our deliveries went there.

Then in 1982 we were granted permission to purchase and erect a 20' x 10' concrete garage in the school grounds. At this point the nuts and bolts of stage construction, scenery etc., at last found a permanent lodging again. Not a resting place, however, as three times a year they are taken out and dusted. Pieces are added and pieces are taken away but always the basics remain.

From this short account, I hope it can be seen that the Society has received help and assistance from many sources outside the Society, for which we will always be indebted.

The Players garage in the school grounds.

Plays performed at The Bateman School

	TITLE	AUTHOR	PRODUCER
1963/64	"The Happiest Days of Your Life"	John Dighton	John Ashton
1964/65	"Wanted One Body"	Raymond Dyer	John Ashton
	"Ladies in Retirement"	E. Percy/R. Denham	Trevor Lancaster
	"Friends and Neighbours"	Austin Steele	Arnold Williams
1965/66	"Flat Spin"	Derek S. Royle	John Ashton
	"A Murder Has Been Arranged"	Emlyn Williams	Trevor Lancaster
	"Beside the Seaside"	Leslie Sands	John Ashton
1966/67	"The Sound of Murder"	William Fairchild	John Ashton
	"Double Trouble"	Michael Brett	John Ashton
1967/68	"Cat Among the Pigeons"	Duncan Greenwood	John Ashton
	"The House on the Cliff"	George Batson	Trevor Lancaster
	"Blithe Spirit"	Noel Coward	Arnold Williams
1968/69	"Lady Killer"	Cyril Campion	Doris Page
	"What's Hatching"	Joan Brampton	John Ashton
	"Dangerous Corner"	J. B. Priestley	Arnold Williams
1969/70	"Busybody"	Jack Popplewell	John Ashton
	"This Happy Home"	Michael Brett	Trevor Lancaster
	"No Time For Fig Leaves"	D. Greenwood/R. King	Arnold Williams
1970/71	"Spring and Port Wine"	Bill Naughton	John Ashton
	"Birthday Honours"	Paul Jones	Doris Page
	"Brief Suspicion"	Patricia Gordon	Arnold Williams

Players' dinner dance c.1966. President Arthur Fryer and Mrs Fryer.

A POTTED HISTORY
PART III: 1971-2000 KNYPERSLEY FIRST SCHOOL

Doris Page

In 1971 we arrived at Knypersley First School. Throughout this time we were, with one or two exceptions, still putting on three plays a season.

For some reason, the middle play, which was usually a drama, always made a loss. Sometimes some of the other plays did too, but not often. As a result of this it was decided to drop the serious play and put on three comedies.

We have put on some very good murder and serious plays since, but not on a regular basis. It was also decided to start the performances from the Tuesday night at a lower rate of admission. This did not help attendances either so after a few years this too was dropped.

We have tried many ways of choosing plays. Any member who found a play which was suitable could bring it to the attention of the others. They could also direct it if they wished.

At one time we met in groups during the summer months for readings. Unfortunately this meant some members did not get a break, and others were away on holiday. We had a scheme whereby six plays were circulated for six players to read. We then met after six weeks, to give our verdict and comment. I found this very boring. I remember my comment on one particular play was "rubbish". Jean Pill was more explicit, she put "bloody rubbish". We have always found group readings much more enjoyable and satisfactory.

We have always felt at home at Knypersley school and we have received lots of help from the headteachers and caretakers. The fire officer used to come and examine the set every play, for fireproofing. On one visit he said that the main curtains were not suitably fireproofed, and if they were not done, we could not 'open'. This was two weeks before the play. Mrs Staniland, the wife of the then Head teacher, hastened to Crewe, to have them attended to. She also returned to collect them when they were ready, in time for the opening night.

On another occasion , Stan Sorby, a leading member of the cast, did not arrive on the opening night. We were very worried and wondered if he had had an accident. At 9.00pm, having had no news, we had to send the audience home. He eventually arrived at 9.30pm and had been at work. When he had told his boss he was in a play, he was asked which was more important, his social or his working life? What could he do?

During this time when Alan Elsmore was President, he and his wife Peggy invited the Players to an 'at home' at their house. This was on the Sunday after Christmas. The conversation centred on over-eating during the festive season and what could we do about it. Rob Pill suggested that we should meet the day after Boxing Day and walk it off. Hence the Christmas walk, known as 'Boxing Day +1' was born. Melva Williams and I thought we were going for a nice gentle walk along country lanes, and turned up in suits, high heels and carrying handbags. It was a bit of a shock to find that we were expected to climb rocks, jump over ditches and generally take part in a mini obstacle course. However, with a little help from our friends, we managed it.

The walk was over the Roaches and of course we had to have a few showers along the way. Cath Gibson was wearing a short anorak and kept complaining that her bottom was wet. However we all enjoyed ourselves.

At the New Year's Eve party, a week later, Ken Tunstall presented Melva and I with cardboard medals. He had painted ladies on them, dressed as we had been, with the words `I did it elegantly.' When I asked about Cath, he presented her with a medal inscribed with "I wet my knickers'.

The walk became an annual event and we also started a summer one. Unfortunately the New Year's party was eventually discontinued. We had had many good times . It was very popular in Biddulph, and the tickets were like gold. It was held at the Biddulph Arms' Hotel. The men would go down the night before to decorate the room with our own garlands. The room looked beautiful. The ladies would blow up balloons and put picture puzzles around the walls. Mrs Moses, the proprietor, put on the most marvellous spread in another room. The music was mainly records but we had a great time.

When Mrs Moses left, the new people wanted the use of the refreshment room, so the food was put in the dancing area. This took up a lot of space. After about three years the hotel changed hands again, and the new tenants were not interested. We did hold it at the Miner's Training Centre for two years but it wasn't the same, newcomers were not interested; the party ceased to be.

We have come a long way since 1950, but there is still need for improvement. Members of the society recently took part in a sponsored Bouncy Castle jump to raise money towards new curtains for Knypersley School. Alan discovered the old winding mechanism we had used at the Gym in his garage. Broken and rusty, it was given to Chris for a clean and overhaul. It is now installed back-stage enabling us to open and close our curtains with ease. We also have had a very good lighting and sound effect system installed by the present headmaster. Our best achievement is the clubroom, a base in which to store our props, hold our committee meetings and our play readings, and of course all our twice weekly play rehearsals.

We recently purchased our own lovely red chairs for the audience, which are very comfortable. However they do have to be transported for every play and returned and stacked very carefully again in our clubroom using our little trolley designed by Ken.

An engrossed audience at Knypersley School.

When we first moved to Knypersley First School we could not use their chairs, as they were too small and unsuitable for adults to sit on for two hours. Consequently, the Sunday before the play, a convoy of private vehicles could be seen wending their way to Woodhouse School in Woodhouse Lane, to collect seventy to a hundred chairs. When Woodhouse were unable to help we borrowed from Bateman School (now Park Middle). All these chairs had to be returned the Sunday after the play.

We have performed quite a few Alan Ayckbourn plays over the years and also tried theatre in the round, with mixed results. Some people liked it, others didn't, for various reasons. I remember one comment was that the lights were too bright and they couldn't eat their toffees!

We have been members of the North Staffs Drama Association for a number of years and have entered several plays for their annual festival. I am proud to say we have won six awards. We had great success with "Relatively Speaking", a play we had previously performed in 1974. In 1996 it was adjudicated, and Dorothy Murdoch received an award for best actress, Peter Murdoch was short listed for best actor and we won an award for best stage presentation and best play in the Festival. It was a marvellous achievement and a very proud moment for us all.

Regarding advertising, over the years we have approached the local papers and radio stations. We used to do a display in the window of the Britannia Building Society until they changed the layout of their premises. We then went to the library where photographs of the cast were displayed along with the story of the current play.

We have sold adverts to local businesses in our programmes. We considered trying to sell season tickets but the scheme was abandoned. We pushed leaflets through letterboxes and have had them positioned in the library and local shops. On one occasion we stood by the Town Hall and tried to sell tickets to passers-by. We have stood outside the supermarkets and once we had the Town Crier calling out for us. Our main form of advertising is our large board in front of Knypersley School, an idea of Rob's which he executes for us.

So we keep marching on. The last fifty years have seen many members come and go but there is no getting rid of me! I don't suppose there are many members today who will be here 50 years hence. I certainly won't! But I like to think that the Biddulph Players will still be active and I wish them all the luck in the world.

"Ours is a Nice House"
Malcolm Haydon, Sylvia Gibson, Julian Hirst, Doris Sabberwal, Alan Elsmore, Harry Morris, Valerie Mellenchip, Alice Ashton, Alan Hart, Rosalind Basson.

"NEW LOOK PLAYERS WERE A HIT"

"A new hall and new faces on stage for Biddulph Players' first production of the season. Producer Doris Page told the Chronicle that the society had been rejuvenated by additions to the acting fraternity, and securing the hall at Knypersley school.

Gertrude Brook was played by Alice Ashton, the perfect choice for the part, which demanded complete melodrama in every line. Her husband Henry, was portrayed by Alan Hart who was suitably henpecked and supressed by his wife.

Seventeen year old Rosalind Basson appearing for the first time, brought a breath of fresh air to the production."

"PLAYERS LATEST WAS WORTH WAITING FOR"

"Waters of the Moon"
Standing: Valerie Mellenchip, Doris Sabberwal, Reg Dunbill, Alan Hart, Malcolm Haydon, Doris Page, Irene Hancock.
Seated: Julian Hirst, Pauline Hill, Sylvia Gibson.

"Listen to that silence"

Alan Hart

John Ashton worked as a porter at Biddulph Grange Hospital where my wife Mary worked as a sister. He was having difficulty casting his production of "Spring and Port Wine" to be performed at Bateman School and heard that I had had some experience of acting with the Methodist Church drama group. I joined the cast for this play in 1970 and can still remember vividly Arnold's portrayal of the upright father who looked after the mill engine. I remember his first lines on stage were "Just listen to that silence". It still remains one of my favourite plays, along with "Strike Happy".

I always enjoy a comedy and a really good laugh and find it very difficult to stop myself laughing, especially on stage when the audience are really enjoying it. It is a great feeling to be suddenly aware of the audience ready to laugh at your every move.

In the "Late Mrs Early", Margaret, being posh, requested no milk in her tea, just lemon. I had then to drop a whole lemon in her cup, splashing tea everywhere. This really made me chuckle and try as I could, I could not keep a straight face or stop my shoulders moving up and down. the audience knew this and laughed even more.

It's always a surprise when an audience does react but very often the reaction is in different places on different nights and can be quite offputting. Many years ago, when dignitaries came on a Friday evening, they rarely laughed and the Players started to call it "kid glove night."

"Strike Happy" was such a humorous play throughout but parts of it were so hilarious. All the men were on strike and under the ladies feet all day, so they too went on strike, leaving the men to fend for themselves. In one particular scene, having had a drink or two, I sat down in the chair and Arnold had to fall on top of me. With Arnold on top of me I took the opportunity to have a really good "belly" laugh, The trouble was Arnold was going up and down with the ups and downs of my stomach, the more the audience laughed the more I laughed. It was all great fun.

In a later scene Arnold had to strip down to his underclothes and climb into a tin bath full of water, which had to overflow once he was seated. All we used was a plastic bag full of water to spill over the sides giving the desired effect. When Arnold's wife Gladys saw it for the first time she was convinced he was stepping into a bath of water and concerned that by the end of the week he would have pneumonia.

I have been known on occasions to miss out some of my lines or go on without my props, my potted geranium in "End of the Honeymoon" and my bottles of beer in the "Late Mrs Early", but it's still all been great fun.

"Sailor Beware"
Standing: Alan Elsmore, Malcolm Haydon, Alan Hart, Alice Ashton, Doris Sabberwal, James McLellan.
Seated: Paulline McLellan, Sylvia Gibson, Margaret Fernyhough.

"Love in a Mist"
Arnold Williams, Jane Sorby, Julian Hirst, Malcolm Haydon, Doris Page, Pamela Brown.

"Big Bad Mouse"
John Gilman, Malcolm Haydon, Jane Sorby, Pamela Brown, Julian Hirst, Doris Page, Hazel Brereton.

John Gilman

"Laughter, it is said is the greatest cure in the world. If this is true Biddulph Players should seriously consider setting up in general medical practice. Indeed, if members of the audience did not find themselves wiping away tears of laughter after every scene, it was certainly not the fault of the actors.

The part of Mr. Bloome, the mouse of the title, was taken by John Gilman. His superb acting was a delight to watch, and made him a leading contender for the star of the production. It must have been far from easy to play this scatter-brained, bumbling character, but John's portrayal was so convincingly and uproariously titillating that it was hard to believe he was not a professional."

"BIDDULPH FARCE WAS ALL GOOD CLEAN FUN"

"I'll Get My Man"
Malcolm Haydon, Alice Ashton, Jane Sorby, Doris Page, Julian Hirst, Sheila Leyland.

"BIDDULPH LAUGHED LAST WEEK IN THE FACE OF ADVERSITY"

"Strike Happy"
Standing: Arnold Williams, Julian Hirst, Alan Hart, Doris Sabberwal, Jane Sorby.
Seated: Sylvia Gibson, Ann Stoddard.

Alan Hart

"Centre pin of the whole action was Alan Hart, who portrayed the weak minded and slow but lovable head of the household, Albert Hellewell. He endeared himself to the large audience from his first entrance to his final exit. His half soaked manner lent itself perfectly to the brand of situation comedy in the play, and some of the predicaments in which he found himself had the audience rolling in the aisles.

During one hectic scene, he himself had great difficulty in keeping his face straight, and at one point broke down in tear-stained laughter, but this did not matter for the audience were with him all the way and they roared even louder.

With the miners of Biddulph joining a strike only hours after the final curtain, the play topically told the hilarious story of the strain of relationships in a family brought about by a strike."

DRAMA BEHIND THE SCENES BUT YOU COULD NOT TELL

This was our first play which required a complete change of scenery. The change was from a bedroom scene performed in front of black curtains. Behind the backdrop a garden scene with patio was to be assembled. To complete the changeover on a small stage with limited access required very precise movement and timing. Then with the help of a very enthusiastic back stage crew and a few rehearsals we managed to complete this, ready for curtain up, in under four minutes.

"After first rehearsals and casting John Ashton was taken ill and Norah Cooke, a friend of the Chairman took over as producer. There was applause from the audience when a drab, untidy flat in the centre of London was transformed to a country garden in the suburbs. The fact is even more creditable when it is considered that behind the stage at Knypersley, there is hardly enough room to swing a cat round on a vertical axis, never mind hunk great pieces of scenery around."

"Relatively Speaking"
Pauline McLellan, Graham Lloyd, Sheila Leyland, Maurice Leyland.

"Crystal Clear"
Margaret McGuire, Doris Page, Stan Sorby, Sylvia Gibson.

Sylvia Gibson

"Despite their newness, and after one or two stumbles, Margaret McGuire and Stan Sorby played the opening minutes - perhaps the most important in any play - with a confidence and zest which belied their inexperience.

Sylvia, who plays the eccentric and fraudulent medium, Mrs Cronely, is a little short of brilliant and is perhaps the leading contender for the 'star of the show' title. Her ability to hold a stage, with the audiences attention with long speeches of magical mumbo jumbo is displayed as she gets right under the skin of the character."

"We Must Kill Toni"
Stan Sorby, Malcolm Haydon, Maurice Leyland, Alan Hart, Susan Smith.

"'TONI' ADDED THE TONIC"

"Brush with a Body"
Standing; Malcolm Haydon, Jane Sorby, Gerald Sheridan, Stan Sorby, Susan Smith, Arnold Williams.
Seated: Doris Page, Margaret Fernyhough, Alice Ashton.

"SOCIETY'S BRUSH WITH A BODY"

"Time and Time Again"
Stan Sorby, Barbara Unwin, Arnold Williams.
Kneeling: Alan Hart, Melva Williams.

"PLAYERS PLEASE, TIME AND TIME AGAIN"

"The cast of Biddulph Player's latest production, 'Time and Time Again' dropped out of their comparatively mundane workaday roles last week and entered the glittering world of show business. The acclaim they received from appreciative audiences every night was just as important to the cast as any oscar or academy award.

For undoubtedly if the town of Biddulph had its own glamorous theatrical award, all cast members would have doubly deserved one. Not many local dramatic society producers would have dared to select this play, but that is reckoning without the ambition of producer Malcolm Haydon."

"Friends and Neighbours"
Standing: Malcolm Haydon, Arnold Williams, Mavis Dunbill, Reg Dunbill.
Seated: Sylvia Gibson, Pauline Hill, Doris Page, Frank Gilmartin.

"DOES BIDDULPH DESERVE ITS DRAMA SOCIETY?"

"Every Biddulph resident must ask itself a very important question this week - does the town deserve its top notch dramatic society? Biddulph Players is acquiring quite a reputation in local thespian circles. Its standards seem to rise with every year and every play that passes. The star of the show was undoubtedly Frank Gilmartin who played the gormless, effeminate, but irresistable Sebastian Green."

"CASTING PROBLEMS WERE JINX ON SEASON OPENING"

"Milk and Honey"
Alan Hart, Margaret Fernyhough, Malcolm Haydon, Cath Gibson, Jane Sorby, Keith Machin

"The Late Mrs Early"
Arnold Williams, Doris Page, Gary Knapper, Ken Tunstall, Christine Koza, Alan Knapper.
Seated: Sylvia Gibson.

"CURTAIN GOES UP BUT NOT IN FLAMES"

"The two members of Biddulph Players who played the parts of father and son in this latest production had a head start. The actors who took the roles of Sam and Terry Early, showed a touch of realism and it was no wonder - they are a flesh and blood father and son! Doris Page as Mrs Early put everything into her performance, which made her the star of the show."

PLAYERS FIND ACCENT IS NO REAL PROBLEM

"There's nowt like a broad Yorkshire accent for bringing out the best in amateur dramatic groups, and a colourful production of 'When we are Married' by Biddulph Players this week is no exception. In fifteen years with the Players, producer Malcolm Haydon has never before had the luxury of hired costumes and a backcloth of excellent props. An authentic peep in the past."

"When we are Married"
Standing; Christine Koza, Stan Sorby, Diane Rowan, Alan Hart, Alice Ashton, Arnold Williams, Howard Evans, Keith Machin, Ken Tunstall.. Seated; Margaret Fernyhough, Gladys Williams, Annette Vallely, Josephine Herbert.

"PLAYERS GAMBLED ON A WINNER"

"Wolf's Clothing"
Kath Hallam, Malcolm Haydon, Jane Sorby, Keith Machin, Diane Rowan, Howard Evans, Doris Page.

"Wedding of the Year"
Derek Heath, Kath Hallam, Sylvia Gibson, Alice Ashton, John Gilman, Cath Gibson, Gwen Stone, Annette Vallely.

Set building

The set design starts as soon as the play is cast. Plans are drawn and ideas sketched. Some furniture items are made in members' garages, others are used from previous sets and repainted in the clubroom.

Three weekends before the play the canvas flats are carried over and assembled on the stage, windows and doors are clamped or nailed and the set created by our team of helpers, painters and decorators. The paint and wallpaper hadly dry the curtains are hung and the scene is set for the first dress rehearsal!

Ken Tunstall, Peter Murdoch, Harry Page and a young helper busy on a new set.

"I do perceive here a divided duty"

Ken Tunstall

My story begins with a wolf cub pack at Biddulph Methodist Chapel. My sons were members, and the Group Scoutmaster had made an appeal for help, so I was assisting Keith Machin to run the cub pack. Through this introduction to Keith my social life was to change in a dramatic way! Keith had connections with Biddulph Players and he encouraged me to go along.

The first part I had was in a play called "The Late Mrs Early". Only a small part and I recall the producer, Malcolm Haydon, asked someone else to stand by in case I didn't make the grade. In this play I was plastered at one point with a large cream cake to the side of my head. I remember the pleasure and fun of acting and the thrill of hearing the audience laugh and enjoy the results of the effort you had put into the performance. So much did I enjoy this first play, when I left the stage I fair rolled down the steps at the rear of the stage with laughter.

Harry Page was the stage manager, as he had been for many plays before, and I couldn't help realising that he was erecting and decorating the set all on his own. Being middle-aged and keen I felt I must offer a helping hand,; actually I think all I did was to fix a handle on a sideboard drawer, but it was to be my initial step into a quarter of a century of set design.

The next play was "When We Are Married" and I had a major part, Albert Parker. Malcolm had warmed to me and thought I was getting better. Again I offered Harry a hand with the set. Somehow I don't remember how, I came to take on the sets and perform on stage as well! It was to set the pattern of things for the next 25 years.

To design a set is rather like painting a picture, you compose a scene to convey to the audience, adding various items to create feeling, depth and realism. It's given me a great deal of pleasure to spend hours doodling, sketching and finally planning out the sets for most of seventy plays. There have been some classics: "Hobson's Choice"; "Outside Edge"; (I nearly got prosecuted over that one) but that's another story; "Relatively Speaking" (the adjudicator was convinced we had a revolving stage), there were two scenes in the play, a bedroom flat and a garden scene and it was changed in minutes; "Barefoot in the Park". "Cure for Love" had four scenes, two with a large bar and two scenes in the family sitting room. You try hiding an 8 feet bar on that stage!

On one occasion I remember a particular lady was required to climb out of a window - she throws the rope out over a convenient beam (all part of the set), ties one end to the radiator, (also part of the set) and lowers herself through the window. As she does so, the radiator becomes dislodged from the wall (all part of the play), water and steam are then supposed to issue forth from broken pipes! Anyway, Alan Hart is in charge of the steam (dry ice) and I am in charge of the spray of water. Well Alan creates so much steam back stage (remember we're in a very narrow passage anyway) that he can't see where to stick his pipe. I have pumped up the large garden spray bottle too much, I give it another couple of pumps, with a huge explosion the plastic bottle rips apart showering water everywhere while the lady is coming through the window upside down, red knickers flying. You see folks, you don't get all the fun!

The ultimate pleasure is in actually performing on stage yourself, there are times when you feel an audience in the palm of your hand and you know they are waiting for your next word - and to deliver that word on time is really a wonderful moment. The emotions that run through the rehearsals and also the week of the play are relived over and over as you remember past plays. My only regret is not starting 25 years earlier than I did.

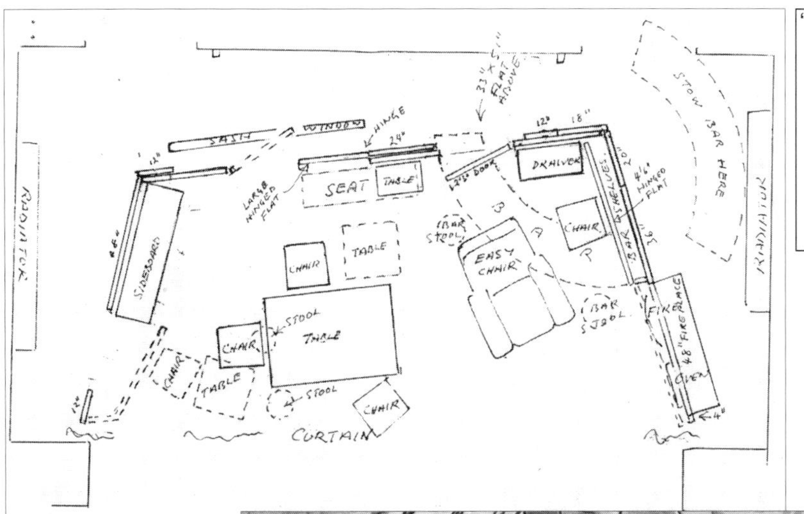

"Cure for Love" stage plan

"The sets are remarkably well designed and constructed considering the confines of a small stage."
There were four complicated scene changes during this play!

Below: A Ken Tunstall painting for a set.

The set for "Tiramisu".

Lighting:
Chris Hirst and Tim Hampton.

Set building:
Ken Tunstall and Graham Bond.

1978 - 79

"Absurd Person Singular"
Standing; Ken Tunstall, Melva Williams, John Gilman, Arnold Williams. Seated: Kath Hallam, Jane Sorby.

Kath Hallam
A sad and suicidal Eva played by Kath Hallam.

"A SINGULAR PERFORMANCE"

"The play opens in the home of Sidney and Jane, and the audience's breath was immediately taken away by the brilliance of the set; one can only marvel at the ingenuity of stage manager, Harry Page and designer, Ken Tunstall. The opening set was the most modern kitchen, complete with fitted cupboards, electric cooker, automatic washer and all mod cons. It was only later that one realised that as the kitchen transformed into the high rise-flat, and later to the Victorian kitchen, each piece of scenery had been so cleverly constructed that it was reversible - the washer turned into a cupboard, the cooker to a fridge, the sink to a fitted wall unit, and so on. The audience was kept waiting only a matter of minutes between sets - a mere hair's breath behind the backdrop were some of the slickest scene changes ever achieved."

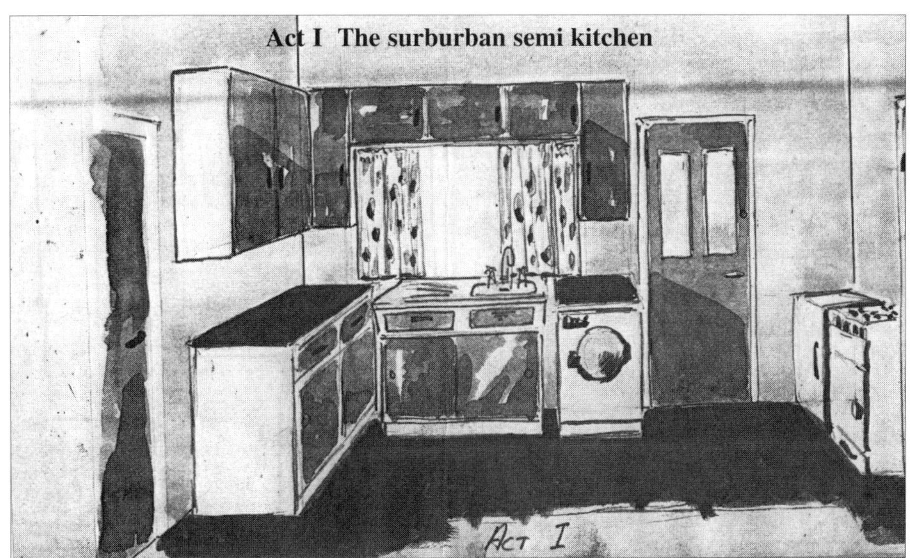

Act I The surburban semi kitchen

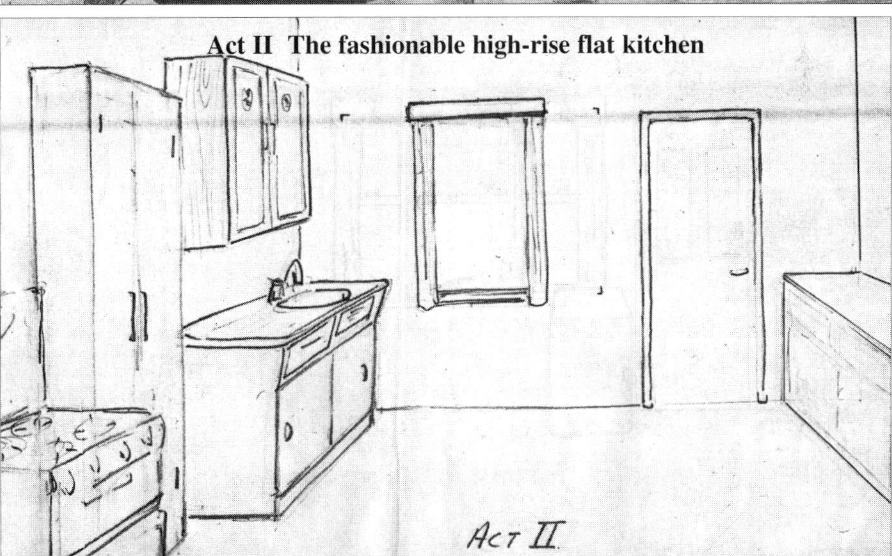

Act II The fashionable high-rise flat kitchen

Act III The Victorian house kitchen

Ken Tunstall's watercolour sketch for the set.

After fifty years of acting, Alice Ashton produced her first play at the age of 72.

"BAD LUCK DOGGED PLAYER'S LATEST PRODUCTION"

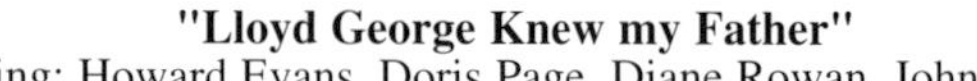

"Lloyd George Knew my Father"
Standing: Howard Evans, Doris Page, Diane Rowan, John Gilman.
Seated: Alan Hart, Josephine Herbert, Robert Pope.

Lucy Milnes

Lucy Milnes, our treasurer for many years, will be well remembered for her numerous acting roles in earlier years.

Sadly she met with a tragic accident on her way home with the 'takings' from 'Lloyd George knew My Father'. She is remembered with great affection for her kindness and meticulous dedication.

"LET'S PRODUCE A PLAY"
(Not so easy, even with 50 years' expertise!)

Dorothy Murdoch

The most difficult job is finding a suitable play and that task starts almost as soon as the previous season comes to its end. Likely producers and interested parties scan play catalogues and investigate the shelves of the County Council Drama Library at Stafford looking for inspiration. At least with library copies you can get a good idea of the suitability of a play and borrow sets for play-reading - quite a few of us know the disappointment of buying a play after reading the enticing catalogue description only to find it fails to come up to expectations.

We are limited by the number, availability, sex and ages of our actors, and the demands of the set (though our designers and set builders have worked wonders many times on our small stage) and fitting in our three productions with the activities of Knypersley First School.

Well, eventually, after a good few evenings of play readings, we come up with a likely candidate or, if we are very lucky, three likely candidates. We choose and confirm our dates, find three producers and before the end of August we are ready to cast our first play. Audition notices are sent out giving details of the characters and the producer turns up at the audition with a small casting committee hoping that enough suitable people will be there to settle the parts that evening. That sometimes happens, sometimes not. I remember with "Last Tango in Whitby" the cast wasn't complete until a couple of weeks before the first night and we had to have a stand-in for Saturday's performance. Anyway, we have always managed to get a full cast eventually; I can't remember having to cancel a production.

So, all cast and into rehearsal, twice a week for about 8 weeks, and now a search for stage manager, prompter, props person, light and sound technicians, wardrobe mistress, make-up expert, front of house staff and refreshment organisers, business manager to organise tickets and programmes and publicity person to make sure lots of people know about it. The secretary has purchased scripts and must obtain a licence from the agent to perform the play and a theatre licence from the local authority to prove the premises are safe for the public.

Rehearsals are held in our clubroom until the week before the play when we rehearse on the stage and for the first time have the correct furniture and doors to open and shut and sound and lighting. All producers try to get the cast to have all their lines learned at least two weeks before the first night so that, with no books in hands, they can get used to handling props and looking at other members of the cast instead of at their books.

Set building starts three weeks before the first night and we are usually able to get into the school at weekends to do this. Occasionally this has not been possible because of the school's own production but then we choose a play with a minimal set which can be built in parts in the clubroom and erected immediately before the dress rehearsal. This is also the time for tickets to be circulated and posters to be displayed, adverts in the press and on local radio and the erection of the advertising board on the outside of the school.

THE WEEK OF THE PLAY ARRIVES! Nervous producer and cast. Dress and technical rehearsals Monday and Tuesday, with press photographers. Hopefully after the weeks of rehearsal we can look forward confidently to Wednesday's opening night. We are ready for our audience to pour in and prove to us through their reactions that all our hard work has been worthwhile.

1979 - 80

"PLAYERS CHOSE A COMPLEX PRODUCTION"

"How the Other Half Loves"
Standing: Melva Williams, Jane Sorby, Alan Hart, Gwen Stone, Robert Pope, Ken Tunstall.

"Tomb with a View"
Jane Sorby, Jim Forster, Bob Hallam, Kath Hallam,
Sylvia Gibson, John Gilman,
Seated: Arnold Williams, Cath Gibson, Doris Page, Annette Vallely.

"KILLING 'EM OFF AT KNYPERSLEY"

"The vultures gather for the reading of a rich old man's will and only horror and blood letting lie ahead for the weird Tomb family. A dotty brother conducting experiments in the east wing; a sister poisoning everyone in sight, and a reincarnation of Julius Caesar, are only three of the lunatic characters. Ken Tunstall succeeds in his first attempt as a producer."

"NEW TALENT IN END OF SEASON PRODUCTION"

"The Devil was Sick"
John Grimwood, Hilda Breeze, Robert Pope, Veronica Brew.
Seated: Gwen Stone, Jim Forster, Barbara Unwin, Ken Tunstall.

Ken Tunstall

"The most outstanding character was the wheel-chair bound Mr Victor Saxton-Hifflish, portrayed excellently by Ken Tunstall. Ken's shrill voice raised in constant complaint typified an awkward old man.

Ken's wife Sheila, became very tired of people saying to her "That's just how he'll be when he's a geriatric, bottom pinching old man!"

"PLAYERS AN UNDOUBTED SUCCESS IN ROMP"

Property mistresses Jean Pill and Peggy Elsmore having a break at the dress rehearsal.

"Two and Two Make Sex"
Melva Williams, Robert Pope, Alan Hart. Seated: Doris Page, Diane Rowan, John Gilman.

"SUCCESS WITH A CHANGE OF PLAY"

"Murder for the Asking"
Pat Gilman, John Grimwood, Jim Forster, Bob Hallam.
Seated: Cath Gibson, Veronica Brew, Ken Tunstall.

"Hobson's Choice"
John Grimwood, Michael Chisnall, Malcolm Tatton, Arnold Williams, John Gilman, Howard Evans.
Christine Robinson, Annette Vallely, Carole Buckley, Barbara Unwin, Christine Koza.

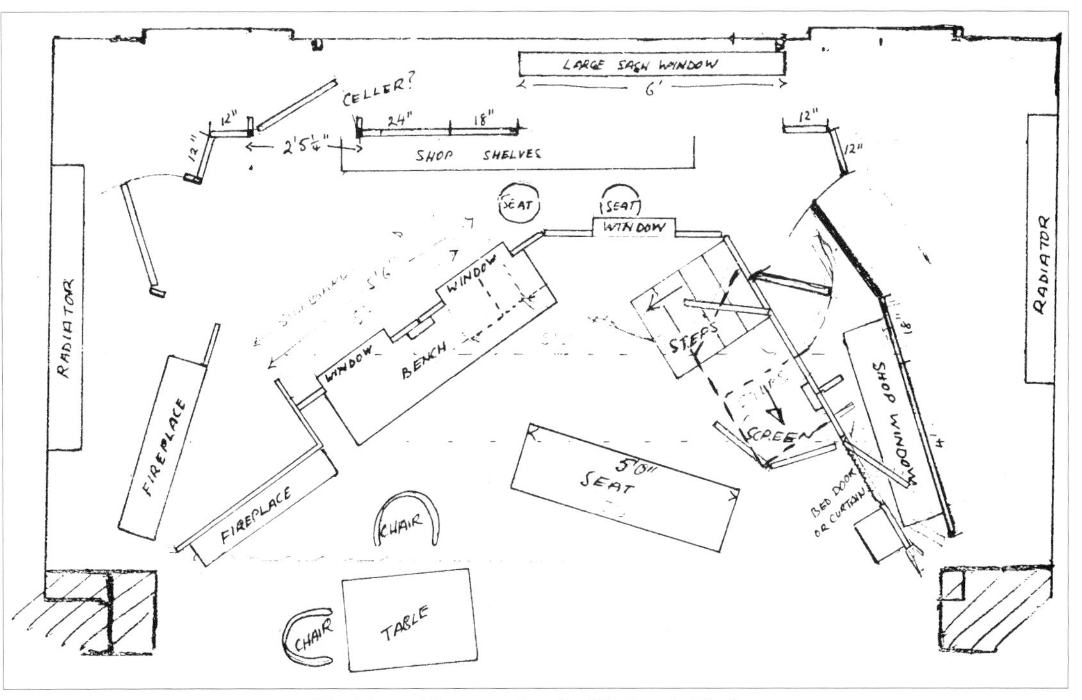

Ken Tunstall's stage plan for "Hobson's Choice.

Interior of Hobson's shop

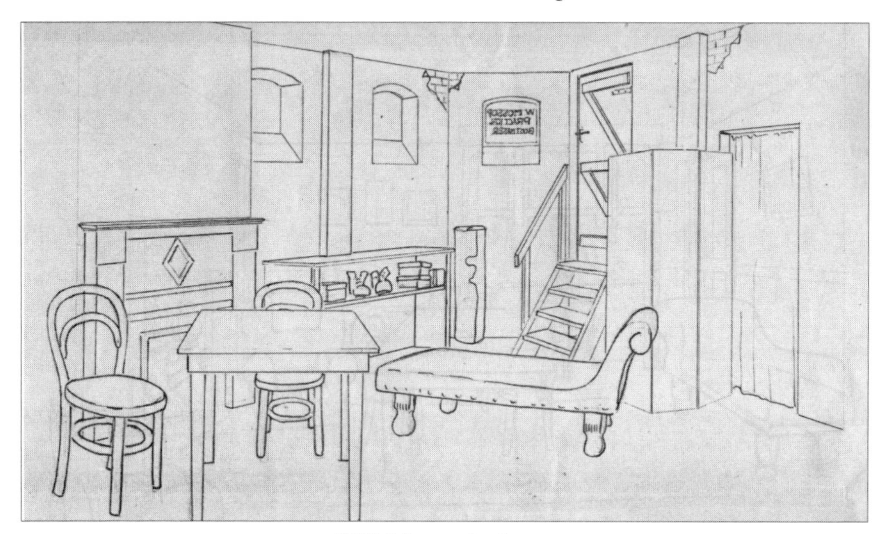

Will Mossop's shop

Living room of Hobson's shop

Cath Gibson - Property mistress

Cath didn't realise when she agreed to be in charge of properties for "Hobson's Choice" that it would become such a challenge.

She discovered a small, old fashioned cobbler's shop in Hope Street where she was able to borrow clogs, lasts, cherry blossom polish tins, old advertisements, a till and a bell for the shop door.

Resisting the temptation to make a cardboard wedding cake, Cath chose to bake and ice her own cake. It was ceremoniously cut by Annette and John at the last night party and consumed by the cast and production team.

John and Annette cutting the cake at the last night party.

Annette Vallely

"The curtains opened, the lights were turned up and the audience were moved to warm applause - and that was only for the set!

Maggie was played magnificently by Annette Vallely. She adopts a clipped Lancashire brogue which makes every utterance an order, a straight backed, no nonsense posture and a tight-lipped stern expression to make Maggie the least endearing heroine ever to win over an audience. What more can be said? She is perfect."

For over twenty years, Annette was a dedicated member of our small group of players, both as an actress and as a producer. Over the years Annette grew in confidence from being a quiet, rather shy person into a self-assured producer of plays.

"ALICE AT 74 IS STILL PRODUCING"

"End of the Honeymoon"
Hilary Moss, Derek Heath, Veronica Brew, Malcolm Tatton, Hazel Bosson, Hilda Breeze.
Seated: Alan Hart, Annette Vallely, John Grimwood

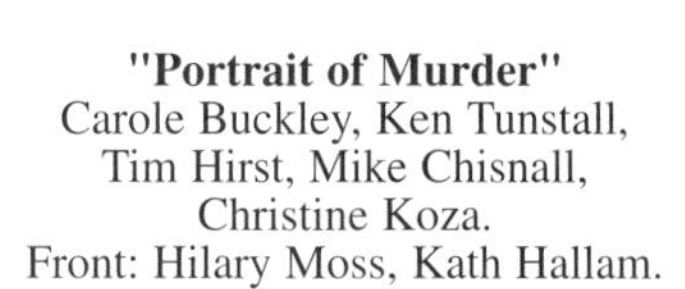

"Portrait of Murder"
Carole Buckley, Ken Tunstall, Tim Hirst, Mike Chisnall, Christine Koza.
Front: Hilary Moss, Kath Hallam.

"KATH'S BIG ROLE IS ANONYMOUS"

"Actress Kath Hallam gave the best performance during the opening of Biddulph Players latest production - yet her name did not even appear in the programme. It was felt that, as the play was so complex, telling the audience Kath's name and role would give the plot away."

Kath Hallam

When it comes to looking the part in a play, amateurs can be just as dedicated as professionals. There are many men in Biddulph today who have grown whiskers in one fashion or another or, conversely, shaved them off, and there are ladies who have changed their hair colour, all in the name of art. So when Portrait of Murder required two ladies to be mistaken for each other, Kath and Hilary wasted no time in visiting the hairdresser!

"Breath of Spring"
Christine Robinson, John Gilman, Chris Middleton, Hazel Bossons, Cath Gibson, Doris Page, Melva Williams.

"SPIRITS ABOUND IN COMEDY"

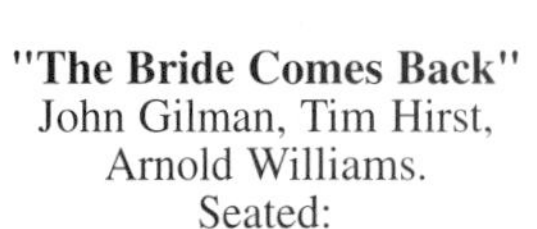

"The Bride Comes Back"
John Gilman, Tim Hirst,
Arnold Williams.
Seated:
Hazel Bosson, Hilary Moss, Doris Page, Christine Robinson, Pat Moore.

"JOURNEY INTO THE UNKNOWN IN MORE WAYS THAN ONE"

"A journey into the unknown faces seven passengers when they step aboard an ocean liner. Six of the roles are men, and this could have caused a problem for producer Arnold Williams. However, the Players were lucky to have six men, including two newcomers, Chris Middleton and Geoff Greatbatch. There is also a newcomer among the women, Pauline Beard."

"Outward Bound"
Howard Evans, Tim Hirst, Chris Middleton.
Seated: Pauline Beard, Geoff Greatbatch, Annette Vallely, Hazel Bosson, Vincent Vodrey.

"STAR ROLE BY CHRIS"

"Mock Orange"
Andrew Unwin, Alan Hart, Pat Gilman, Chris Middleton, Geoff Greatbatch.
Seated: Sue Hargreaves, Josie Herbert, Barbara Unwin, Hilary Moss.

Prompting

Cramped into a tiny space in semi-darkness sits the prompter glued to their book, never seen and never heard - hopefully.

A momentary lapse in concentration and the actors have jumped a few pages ahead and a cue is lost! If an experienced actor realises in time and picks up the cue, no one will notice. Once the place is lost a whole scene might be repeated. It could end in chaos. It is all your fault!

If you are at the side of the stage and are visible to the cast you may have little to do but mouth a word; but sometimes you cannot be seen, as in a bedroom scene when you have no way of knowing if a pause is the result of a passionate embrace - or the need for a prompt!

Louise Unwin - Prompter

"A DIFFICULT FISH FOR PLAYERS TO LAND"

"Three shady characters search a hotel for a hidden suitcase full of cash."

"Off the Hook"
Ken Tunstall, Vincent Vodrey, John Grimwood, Howard Evans, John Gilman.
Seated: Hazel Bosson, Pat Moore, Annette Vallely, Barbara Unwin, Christine Robinson.

"REFRESHING CHANGE FOR THE PLAYERS"

"Barefoot in the Park"
Doris Page, Alan Hart, Ken Tunstall.
Seated: John Gilman, Chris Middleton, Melva Williams.

John Gilman and Stuart Shingler in control of lights and sound.

Lighting

Lighting is an essential part of any production if a good atmosphere is to be created on the stage. Electrical knowledge combined with an artistic ability makes an ideal lighting man. The lights and wiring have, until very recently, had to be taken down at the end of each play and put up again when needed. This is a long procedure, especially when certain techniques are required and can only be set up in the dark. Good lighting often goes unnoticed. Poor lighting, unfortunately, is often commented upon.

"The White Sheep of the Family"
John Grimwood, Alan Hart, Howard Evans, Peter Murdoch. Seated: Dorothy Murdoch, Pat Gilman, Cath Gibson, Chris Middleton.

"JITTERY START BUT SHOW LOOKS A HIT"

"SUCCESSFUL START TO PLAYERS NEW SEASON"

"Ladies in Retirement"
Debbie Austin, Annette Vallely, Leigh Colclough, Clara Heyhoe.
Seated: Dorothy Murdoch, Hilary Moss, Doris Page.

"A CURE FOR THE BLUES BY BIDDULPH PLAYERS"

"The scene the Flying Shuttle public bar; the audience are introduced to the wizened Mrs Doorbell. Hilary Moss nearly steals the show as the bitter scrounging old woman whose wrinkled stockings would put Nora Batty to shame! She has the audience in hysterics when she blows her nose on a handkerchief she keeps up her knicker leg!"

"Cure for Love"
Leigh Colclough, Hazel Bosson, Geoff Greatbatch, Robert Pope, John Gilman, Howard Evans.
Seated: Debbie Austin, Hilary Moss, Dorothy Murdoch, Estelle Wright, Pauline Beard

Biddulph Players Amateur Dramatic Society
presents:-
"The Cure For Love"
by WALTER GREENWOOD
on Saturday 9th February 1985
in the
Knypersley First School, Newpool Road
at 7-30 p.m.
Tickets £1-00 Refreshments available

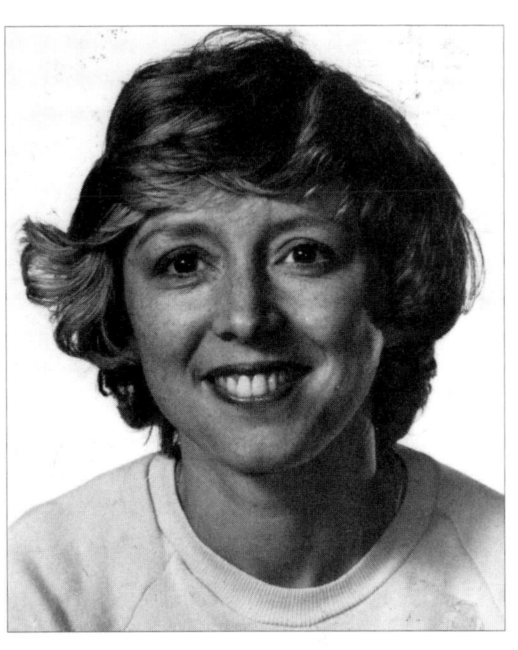

Hilary Moss

As the wizened, old, Mrs Doorbell, Hilary achieved her new look with the aid of rice krispies glued to her face to resemble warts. They looked and felt so awful, Debbie Pedley, our make-up artist, couldn't bear to touch them.

"TALENT SHINES THROUGH IN BIDDULPH DRAMA"

"Dark Lucy"
Michael Lightfoot,
Geoff Greatbatch.
Barbara Unwin, Hilary Moss,
Pat Gilman.

The Campaign for the Club-House

Robert H. Pill

During the three and a half years, March 1983 to September 1986, in my period as Chairman, an undercurrent of high drama permeated the meetings of the Players' Committee. The news had trickled through, per Councillor George Humphries I think, that the old woodwork block at Knypersley First School was on the cards for demolition. We thereupon embarked on a campaign of correspondence, telephone calls and meetings with the County Education and Estates Officers to try to secure its use for the Players.

From the first our application was treated sympathetically but predicted costs of £800 per annum rental plus a substantial repair, improvement and maintenance bill could, it seemed, place it beyond our reach, particularly since it appeared that no 'discretionary relief' would be available on the projected rates bill of £200 from Staffs Moorlands District Council despite the fact that *"....Biddulph has no commercial theatre or cinema, no publicly provided or sponsored club for local arts..."* Nevertheless the terms of lease offered by the County Education Committee were accepted in principal in the hope that a substantial reduction of the rental would finally be achieved.

The only means of achieving a rates reduction was, it appeared, through the registration of the Society as a Charity and after preliminary contact with the Charity Commission this was put in motion with the supply of copies of our constitution, annual accounts, committee minutes, scrap book excerpts, etc.

Then came an unexpected body-blow with the news of a County cost-cutting exercise which implied that the Players' use of the school and its stage would be restricted to ONE EVENING a week. We reacted to this energetically with letters to the County, our MP, David Knox, the local press councillors, etc. gaining a great deal of publicity and a County Education Office press release raising the ante to TWO evenings a week with increased rental charges! We did in due course regain our 6-night hire but too late to enable our first play of the 1985-86 season to be put on.

Meantime, examining our finances, we decided that our upper limit for annual expenditure on rent, rates, gas, etc, must be contained within £400 and to manage this we should have to double members' subscriptions and increase the price of tickets to our plays by probably 20%. This information plus recent Statements of Account were passed, after our 1985 AGM, to the County Clerk, from whom the whisper came through subsequently, confirmed in the 'Chronicle' that the property was to be formally transferred from the Education Committee to the Libraries, Arts and Archives Committee. They set a rent to the Players of £50 per annum for a period of five years - a wonderfully successful conclusion to a long period of negotiation and clear evidence of support and goodwill from County Hall to whom the society remains indebted.

Registration of the Players as a Charity (No. 518204) was finally achieved after the revision of our Constitution at our AGM September 1986 and the remission of our rates bill by SMDC followed. During the preceding summer our task force of members had laid on gas and electricity supplies, carried out essential repairs and redecorated the premises (paint courtesy of Dulux Community Scheme) to achieve the splendid club room we now enjoy.

Right:
The Players' clubroom, venue for our meetings and rehearsals.

Below:
Geoff, Brian and Steve renovating the interior of the clubroom.

Above: Old toilet wing

Left:
Dorothy and Peter Murdoch and Margaret Fernyhough rehearsing in the Club Room with Ken Tunstall behind and Leigh Colclough far left scratching his head.

"One man in his time plays many parts"

Leigh Colclough

On a cold winter's night in 1984 a lady I was working with at the time approached me and said , "Leigh we are desperate for a man." My face lit up, it was unaccustomed music to my ears. "For a play" she said. I suddenly felt deflated; nevertheless I reluctantly went along and to my surprise I was cast as Albert Feather in "Ladies in Retirement". It started a fifteen year association with the Players which has given me some of the most enjoyable times I have ever had - with my clothes on that is!

Over the years I have worked with some very special people, acting, directing and helping to build the sets for many of our productions. No matter what has happened at work or at home I have had the chance to forget it all for an hour or two, to be someone else. It's great therapy.

In my time I have been a teacher, dentist, cricketer, rugby player, policeman and a funeral director to name but a few. Married at least a dozen times and had enough children to fill a Barnardo's Home. Where else could you do that and stay out of the Sunday papers?

The part which I enjoyed playing most of all was Billy Fisher in "Billy Liar". The role which caused most amusement, to my friends that is, was my portrayal of Bobby Franklyn in "Run for your Wife". My performance of a 'gay' person so upset a transexual member of the audience, who stormed out of the hall, slamming all the doors!

Being part of Biddulph Players Golden Anniversary celebrations means something very special to me. It's given me the opportunity to live out some of my dreams, to be famous for a week or so each year. It's an interest I can still participate in when I'm old and grey, hopefully, who knows what the future will bring. Here's to another great fifty years.

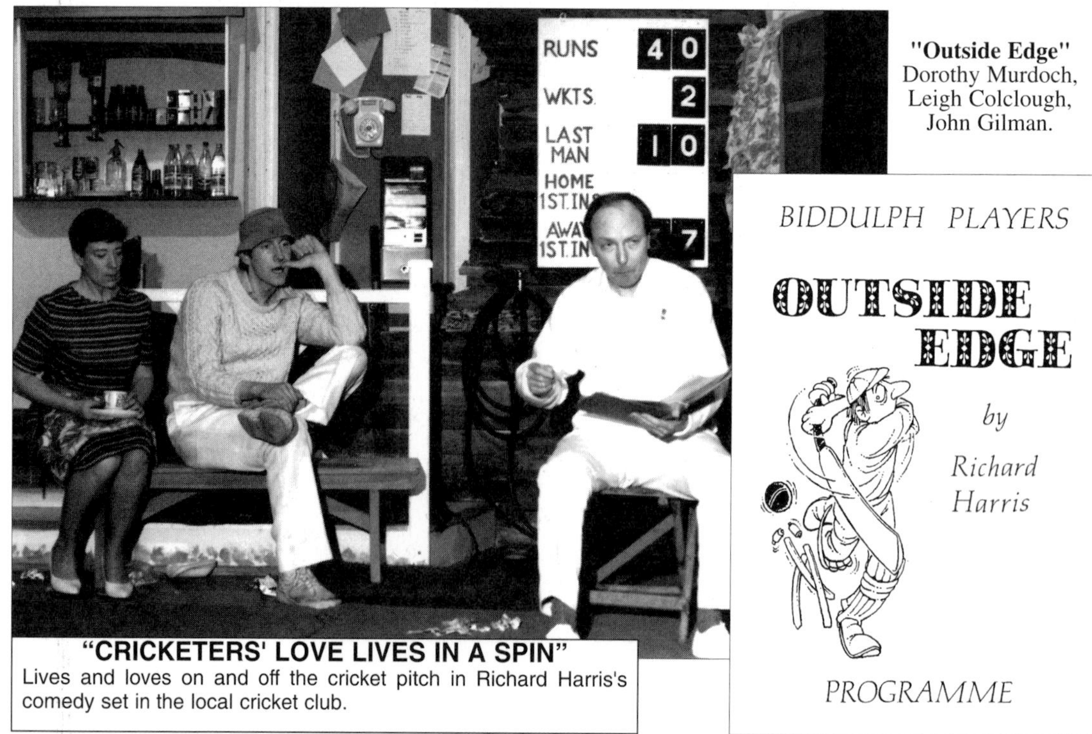

"Outside Edge"
Dorothy Murdoch, Leigh Colclough, John Gilman.

"CRICKETERS' LOVE LIVES IN A SPIN"
Lives and loves on and off the cricket pitch in Richard Harris's comedy set in the local cricket club.

John Gilman making a sound recording for the cricket match in "Outside Edge"

STAGE MANNERS ARE IMPECCABLE

The first play of the Norman Conquest Trilogy by Alan Ayckbourn. All the plays occur during a single weekend set in the same house with the same cast.

"Table Manners"
Peter Murdoch, Ken Tunstall.
Seated: Christine Robinson, Pauline Beard, Geoff Greatbatch, Hilary Moss.

"Perchance to dream"

Peter Murdoch

I joined an Amateur Dramatic Society over thirty years ago. I had always been interested from the times when I went as a boy with my mother to watch the village group. Later I also thought that appearing on stage might give a shy chap like me some added confidence when going for interviews for jobs, or when talking to people. It worked to some extent I suppose, but I am still a quiet sort of person. Now I like nothing more than taking on these other roles so that I can pretend to be someone more exciting.

It took me quite a few seasons before I was given a part, and I was almost on the point of giving up. Then, because I was in digs with a Swiss chap, I was able to give a better reading using a German accent than anyone else in the group. I got the part. That is when I found that there is more to acting than learning the lines and saying them at the right time.

To give a convincing performance you must think what sort of a voice the character needs, how the character might walk, how he might use his hands. The script should help and give some guidance, but when you walk on that stage on the first night you are not yourself. Somehow between the first rehearsal and the dress rehearsal you must have transformed yourself. All this I learned from the director of that first play. I might have had a convincing accent, but he kept telling me to growl as I said my lines - his way of getting me to use a deeper voice I guess. He kept telling me to stand straight with my nose in the air - his way of getting me to look more in control of the situation. I learned a lot from him.

Now I like to start with the way a character might speak and quickly move on to how he might walk - does he lead from the feet, knees, stomach, chest, shoulders or head.? Trying these alternatives can lead one more easily into the character. I like to add in any gestures and hand movements once the rehearsals are 'without books'.

In addition to telling you where on stage you should move, the play director can give you guidance in character building if he thinks you need help with your attempts, but at the end of the day it is you who are doing the acting.

After being involved with six other societies in other parts of the country I came to join Biddulph Players. This was after sharing the stage with one of it's members in a pantomine in Congleton - she was the principal boy, I was the dame. That was about fifteen years ago and my first play was called "White Sheep of the Family". Since then I have been fortunate to have been able to play a great variety of roles, including a repeat of that chap with the German accent, Herr Winkelkopf, from the very first play I did!

In my early years I was able to play young men , middle aged and old men, now sadly as the years pass the opportunity to play the young juvenile lead has also passed.

I can dream though. Do any of you remember how I, as Norman, rolled on the carpet with my wife, or went off for a dirty weekend with my wife's sister, or comforted her brother's wife over the dinner table. That was in the three plays that were the "Norman Conquests."

I had two wives in "Run for your Wife". I have bared my bum in "Up and Under"; I guess there isn't a lot that I haven't tried. But I am sure there are still countless challenges still waiting for me out there and I await them eagerly.

"As an unperfect actor on the stage."

Melva Williams

My memories of the time I spent with Biddulph Players are many and varied and I can still laugh out loud recalling incidents at rehearsal and in actual performance. Laughing during a performance was always frowned on, particularly by Alice Ashton and more particularly if she was the producer of the play in question.

I remember appearing on stage one night as the hostess of a party whose guests included Doris Page and the incomparable Alan Hart. There were at least six of us on stage, Doris seated down left, me standing on the right offering nuts to everyone, and Alan centre stage sitting on the settee - and he was so relaxed, so comfortable and at ease, smiling affably and nodding in agreement whenever anyone spoke. He continued to nod and smile during a very awkward few minutes when every other member of the cast was aware that he should in fact have been speaking a line. We all looked. The prompter prompted, to no avail. I moved closer with my nuts and half turning from the audience, muttered the line under my breath. Alan took a nut and ate it and nodded and smiled. He clasped his hands together, thrust them between his knees, swayed back and forth and smiled. I caught his eye, fixed him with a stare, and nodded to him meaningfully. Suddenly realisation dawned. He lurched forward where he was sitting and bellowed, "Oh, I met Bobby Charlton once", then he chuckled and he twinkled, and though I had only to reply "During the war?" I could not. I fixed my gaze on the dish in my hand, I willed myself not to laugh, but I really knew I was lost. So I glanced at Doris; she would be steely-eyed, a look of disapproval on her face. She would save me. But Doris was a quivering heap, the sherry in the glass on her knee threatening to spill over on her dress; the rest of the cast stood with bowed heads and shoulders that shook uncontrollably. The tears ran down my face, I tried several times to say my line and only managed it falteringly on the fourth attempt. I have no idea how we managed to get through the rest of the scene. Afterwards Alice was livid and called us a bunch of amateurs but the audience loved it and the memory of it will stay with me and gladden my heart forever.

There are other memories; of Arnold Williams who picked up and started to eat the last piece of Battenburg cake on the plate at the very moment that I reached for it to say my line, "This cake is stale, I shan't go there any more". I don't think Gladys had given him any dinner that night; of Trevor Lancaster, in his evening suit, a cocktail shaker in his hand, the contents running down his sleeve as he spoke his lines; of Cath Gibson cracking her head on the sash window because she forgot to duck as she entered the room, and of Millicent Hurst, who began the week with a very small part of a maid, and who added so many lines and bits of business each night that by the end of the week she practically had a leading role. I remember shouting "Knickers!" having just bitten off a chunk of raw carrot, and spraying everyone on the front row. I have been stuck backstage unable to make an entrance because someone skipped a page and suddenly we were into another scene entirely; I have been stuck on stage with a 40 inch bust (not my own), unable to make an exit for precisely the same reason. I have spent countless hours locked in my loo learning my lines; I have felt physically sick each time the curtain opened and the national anthem played, but to perform on a stage is a magical thing and for me nothing else could ever match up to it.

"BIDDULPH PLAYERS ENJOY SOME NAUGHTY ROMPS"

The second of the trilogy with naughty Norman planning an illicit weekend.

"Living Together"
Peter Murdoch, Pauline Beard, Christine Robinson, Hilary Moss, Ken Tunstall, Geoff Greatbatch.

"PLAYERS EXCEL WITH ANSWER TO DYNASTY"

Hilarious comedy, set in the late 1960s, centres round Mum's fortieth anniversary as she manipulates and bullies her three sons.

"The Anniversary"
Peter Murdoch, Robert Pope, Andrew Unwin, Claire Nicholls, Doris Page, Raquel Gascon.

"PLAYERS SHOW LIFE IN MODERN MIDDLE AGES"

Three middle-aged couples going through a mid-life crisis, their hopes and dreams shattered.

"Middle-age Spread"
Leigh Colclough, John Gilman, Ken Tunstall.
Catherine Biddulph, Dorothy Murdoch, Linda Hargreaves.

Props

Something you happily take on and then discover how difficult it is going to be! How do you find a fondue set? How do you make a realistic looking whisky which someone can be seen to drink with great relish? Serving meals can sometimes cause difficulties as Sheila Tunstall discovered in this play by Alan Aykbourn. The plot is set at a dinner party in the present. It has ten scenes, four of which centre around the dinner party and the same meal. They are interspersed with a series of flashbacks as the characters unfold.

Andrew Unwin helping backstage ate six desserts each evening so that it looked as if a meal was in progress. One props lady once made some sandwiches for the dress rehearsal and the poor cast were still eating the same plate of sandwiches on the last night!

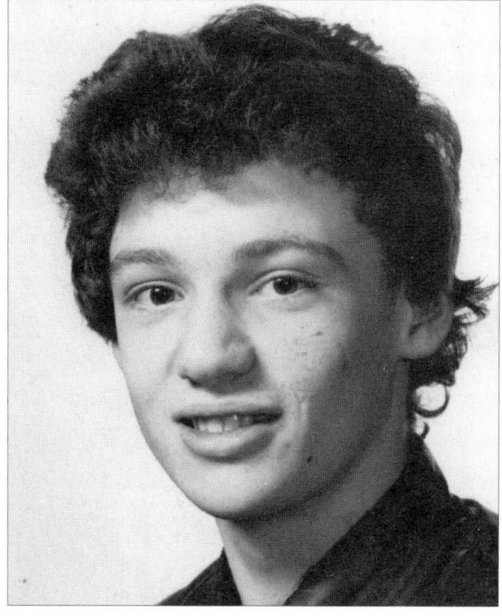

Andrew Unwin

BIDDULPH CARNIVAL

Doris Page and Dorothy Murdoch as the `Keystone cops' c.1987.

Biddulph Players' float 'Silent Movies' in Biddulph Carnival c.1987.

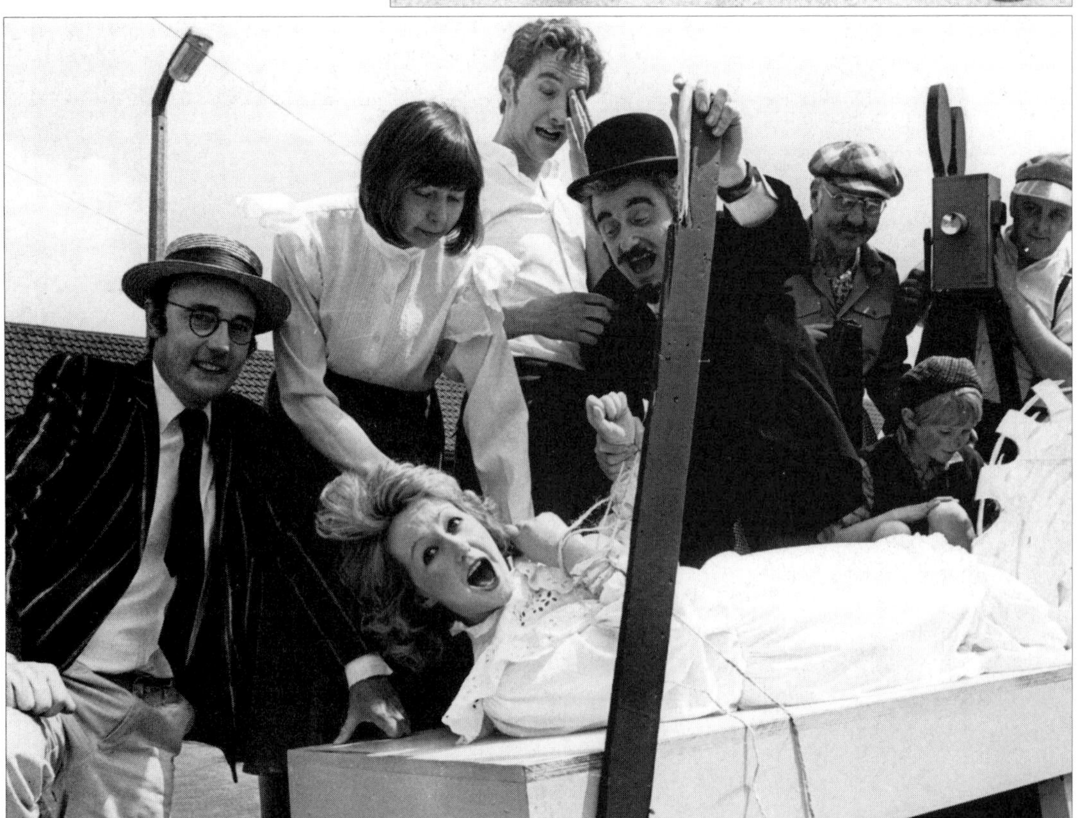

THE GRANGE OPEN DAY

Pat Gilman as Queen Victoria with husband John, son Craig and daughter Claire inside the Grange 1988.

Kath Hallam and Ken Tunstall as Mr and Mrs Bateman raising funds for Biddulph Grange Gardens 1988.

"YOUNG BILLY IS THE PERFECT LIAR"

Billy, the undertaker's clerk, bored with his North Country family background, takes refuge in his own invented world.

Leigh Colclough

"Leigh has a wonderful range of effective facial expressions and animated mannerisms. His acting is excellent and his timing impeccable. The role might almost have been written for him."

"Billy Liar"
Peter Murdoch, Louise Unwin, Andrew Unwin,
Claire Nicholls, Pauline Beard.
Leigh Colclough, Pat Gilman, Ruth Gower.

Pat Gilman

"The play opens on a stereo-typical working class household, with the grandmother played by Pat Gilman - who gives solid support throughout - muttering into the fireplace as she sucks sweets."

"THIS SHORT PLAY IS LONG ON LAUGHS"

A play within a play, with people being bumped off at an alarming rate."

"Farndale Murder Mystery".
Pat Moore, Dorothy Murdoch,
Christine Robinson, Catherine Biddulph.
Pat Gilman, Ruth Gower, Janet Shingler.

"Round and Round the Garden"
Geoff Greatbatch, Ken Tunstall,
Peter Murdoch, Chris Robinson.

"PLAYERS STAGE FINAL CONQUEST"

The final play in the Norman Conquest's Trilogy by Alan Ayckbourn.

Mary Hart

"There Goes the Bride" was the only play Mary appeared in. Although her performance was good Mary decided that her talents lay in another direction. So, for over twenty years she became the mainstay of Biddulph Players where she directed and produced the refreshments for all our productions.

Working continuously for many years as our social secretary and fund raiser, Mary left her mark and consequently, a gaping hole when she was subsequently taken ill.

"LAUGHTER ALL THE WAY"

The hapless attempts of an affluent London family to get their daughter to the church on time.

"There Goes the Bride"
Claire Nicholls, Mary Hart, Alan Hart, Margaret Fernyhough, Leigh Colclough
Ken Tunstall, Peter Murdoch, Louise Unwin.

"ACCENT ON THE ABSENT FRENCH"

A saucy comedy set in the hotel room of a French village. Everyone in the wrong bed, seductions and confrontations run rampant!

"Bedfull of Foreigners"
Hilary Moss, Arnold Williams, John Gilman, Leigh Colclough, Dorothy Murdoch, Peter Murdoch, Jane Parkin.

Changing sets

Top right: John having problems with THE radiator. During one performance he was unable to untie the rope to the beam above - unfortunately Dorothy was hanging on the other end! Eventually he did manage to undo the knot, but even a short pause seems a long time when you're on stage in a sweat!

"PLAYERS PLEASE, TIME AND TIME AGAIN"

Popular Acykbourn comedy. The antics of womaniser Graham and his brother-in-law Leonard, who holds conversations with the garden gnome. Popular Acykbourn comedy.

"Time and Time Again"
Peter Murdoch. Seated: Louise Unwin, Ken Tunstall, Dorothy Murdoch. Leigh Colclough.

"BIDDULPH PLAYERS STAGE FINE COMEDY"

A bedroom farce in a highly ingenious and original setting, in which all the rooms, passages and stairs are on a single level.

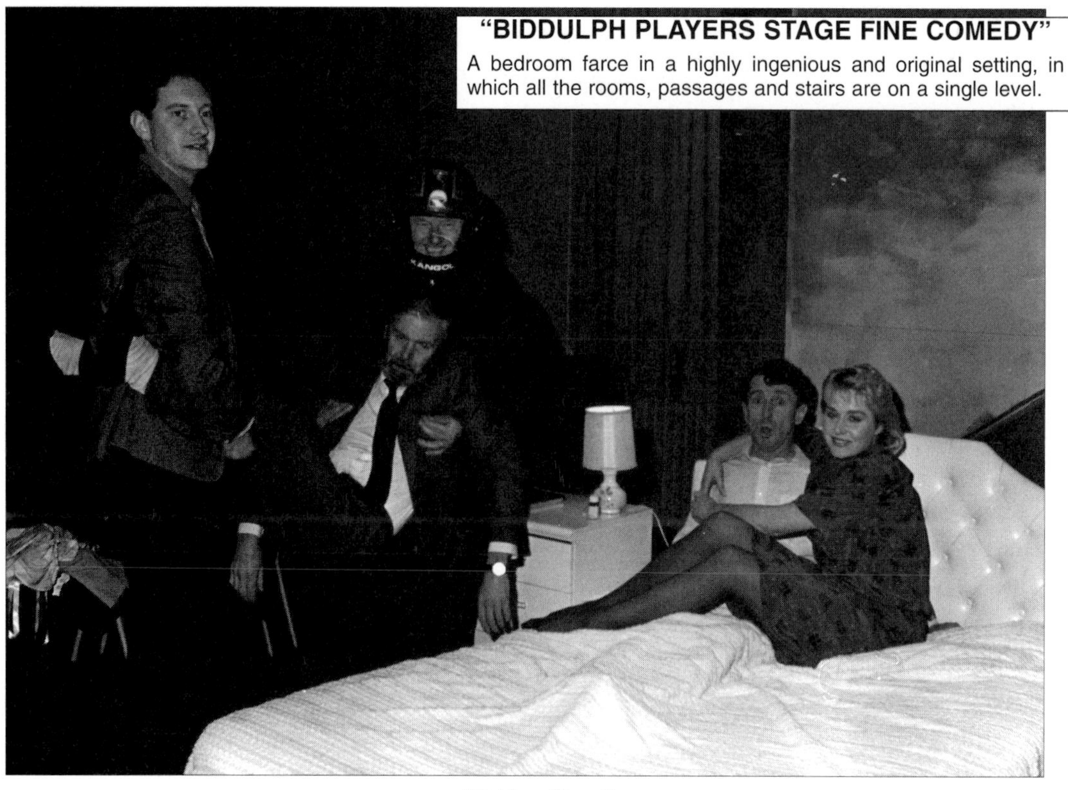

"Taking Steps"
Leigh Colclough, Ken Tunstall, Ron Tweats.
Peter Murdoch, Louise McIntyre.

Progamme cover designed by Craig Gilman.

Kelly Snape

Kelly played the part of Carol in "Our Day Out"

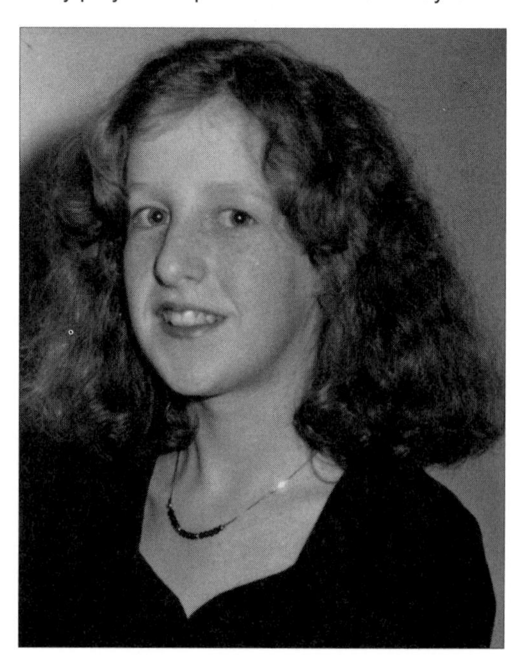

"PLAYERS' OUTING THAT'S A LITTLE DIFFERENT"
"Our Day Out". Willy Russell's challenging comedy centred round a school trip to Conway Castle.

"Our Day Out"
Dee Lapsley, Ayza Beard, Craig Gilman. Lesley Ann and Simon Shinglet, Ann Rowley, Laura Jones. Mark Hurst, Claire Gilman, Alison Colclough. Pauline Beard, Ken Tunstall, Damon Beard.

"PLAYERS MIS-TIME TRIP FROM MARS"
The hapless attempts of the 'Farndale amateur dramatic group' to stage a science fiction thriller.

"They Came From Mars"
Catherine Biddulph, John Gilman, Dorothy Murdoch, Doris Page, Pat Gilman.

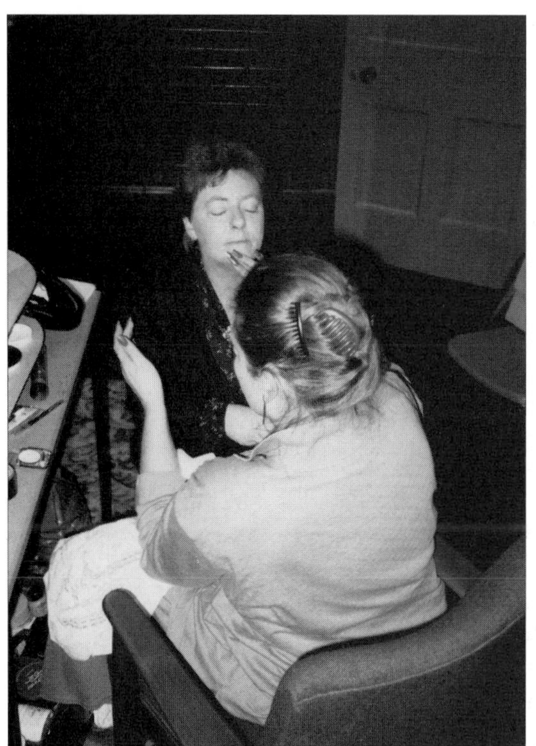

Debbie Pedley

Our make-up artist Debbie Pedley putting the finishing touches to Pat.

Theatre in the Round

Lighting was undoubtedly the biggest problem. The roof of a P.E. hall does not lend itself to the positioning of the extra lighting required to illuminate the scene from all directions and a scaffolding tower had to be hired for the lighting engineer to fix overhead bars to mount the lights.

Then it was very difficult to satisfy the fire officer with the seating arrangements - we had to make many changes before we got the licence.

The costume, stage dressing and props had to be precise in every detail, from the ceremonial serving of tea, the stationery and pens, to the champagne. Each night the borrowed props had to be carefully wrapped to secure them before the furniture could be lifted onto the stage.

In the end the production was a real 'tour de force' for everyone concerned.

"PLAYERS' PIECE THEIR MOST SIGNIFICANT"

Set in the late nineteenth century, Frank Harvey has adapted this poignant love story written by Thomas Hardy.

"Day After the Fair"

Jenny Hall, Ken Tunstall, Trevor Brignall, Mark Hurst. Dorothy Murdoch, Doris Page, Claire Wilshaw.

"BIG ROLES FOR FOUR"
Two couples in a knockabout farce, by Joyce Rayburn, set in a North London house.

"Don't Start Without Me"
Melva Williams, Louise Unwin. Jonathan Hurst, Mark Hurst.

"SHOCKS AND WRY HUMOUR GALORE FOR PLAYERS"
An attempt to plagiarize an unknown dramatist's thriller takes a sinister turn.

Ira Levin's "Death Trap"
Dorothy Murdoch, Pat Gilman, Alan Hart. Seated: John Gilman, Peter Murdoch.

Front of House

Robert H. Pill

Casting, producing, stage construction, stage management, make-up, costume, the provision and organisation of 'properties' are the fundamental elements of play production of which the public see nothing except the dramatic results on the stage itself.

The front of house staff are the welcoming face, the contact with and hosts of the public as they enter, seek their seats and finally depart after the show. Front of house duties in our small Biddulph school theatre, perhaps more involved than in many modern premises, commence with barrowing in and placing of the auditorium seats in precise rows (always subject to final check by KT) the setting out of tables for the sale of sweets and refreshments, tickets and programmes. All curtains are drawn, emergency exit lighting switched on, the refreshment tables set with sufficient cups, etc to satisfy interval requirements.

Public reception commences with our man, in dinner jacket, at the ticket table after which all must run the gauntlet of our young ladies (black skirt, white blouse) as they offer to sell programmes, sweets, tickets for tea or coffee. tickets for the interval raffle before exhausted, they are able to select and recline in the seat of their choice.

Meantime, other smartly dressed ladies are setting water to boil, opening packets of biscuits next door whilst up in the new control box, music is switched on and finally, as entrance doors are closed and curtained of, they are able to dim off the auditorium lights and let the play commence

Interval time, refreshments served, raffle winners drawn and prizes awarded, cups cleared for the wash up, on to the final act and time for the departure, all we hope, cheered and enlivened by what they have seen and heard, looking forward to the next production by the Biddulph Players.

Property assistants meantime are tidying up the stage, reorganising their props, 'Front of House' clean up the hall and unless we are fortunate enough to be operating during a school holiday week, man(and woman)-handle the 100 chairs for overnight storage on the stage, restack the tables, draw the curtains to leave all in perfect readiness for the scholars next morning.

Rob Pill

With the built in conviction that the stage was no place for him, Robert Pill still felt sure that this little group of actors and drama enthusiasts were worthy of all the support he could give them.

Since joining the society in 1958 he has taken on various managerial posts, including business manager, secretary, subscription secretary, chairman and latterly, front of house duties.

In 1999, Rob and his wife Jean were made life members in honour of all the work they have put in.

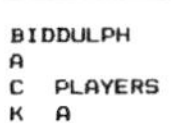

BIDDULPH
A
C PLAYERS
K A
G
E

And so we come to to the final play for this season with a presentation from Alan Ayckbourn's trilogy "The Norman Conquests". The other two titles "Table Manners" & "Living Together" where staged by us last season. Each play is a story in its own right even though the action takes place simultaneously and with the same characters. It had been hoped to use the same players in the same roles for this third part of the trilogy but due to other commitments this has proved impossible.

There are no new faces this time but we are sure you will enjoy watching the old -oops familiar ones

THANKYOU FOR YOUR CONTINUED SUPPORT - WE LOOK FORWARD TO SEEING YOU AT THE START OF OUR NEW SEASON IN NOVEMBER.

ALSO OUR GRATEFUL THANKS TO ANYONE WHO HAS HELPED IN ANY WAY WITH THIS PRODUCTION.

Special thanks to Knypersley Garden Centre for the garden greenery - excluding nettles and brambles.

- HAVE A SAFE JOURNEY HOME -

BIDDULPH PLAYERS

ROUND AND ROUND THE GARDEN

ALAN AYCKBOURN

Programmes, tea ladies and chairs.

Right: On tea and refreshments, Doris Page, Shirley Fitchford and Cath Gibson.

Below: Our luxury chairs and the special chair trolley made by Ken Tunstall.

"PLAYERS SHINE IN THEATRE CLASSIC"

Kesselring's classic comedy is set in Brooklyn and evolves round the kindly `deeds' of two elderly spinster sisters.

"Arsenic and Old Lace"

Robert Walker, Leigh Colclough, David Adey, Jonathan Hurst Ken Tunstall, John Gilman, Lesley Ann Shingler, Kevin Knapper, Peter Murdoch, Alan Hart. Seated: Melva Williams, Arnold Williams, Doris Page.

"PLAYERS IN WORLD OF EDDIE WARING"

John Godber's comedy set in the North of England centres on the `Wheatsheaf Arms' amateur rugby team and their pride in an unbroken record of defeat.

"Up and Under"

Peter Murdoch, Mark Hurst, Chris Middleton, Ken Tunstall. David Weatherall, Louis McIntyre, Leigh Colclough.

"CONFESSIONS OF A SHADY LADY"
Adapted from "Les Enfants d'Edouard" by Marc-Gilbert Sauvajon and Frederick Jackson and set in Paris.

"Dear Charles"
Ken Tunstall, Janet Shingler, Leigh Colclough, John Gilman, Peter Murdoch, Simon Shingler, Ian Bostock, Dorothy Murdoch, Lesley Ann Shingler.

Carnival Day
Peter Murdoch, Pauline Beard and family, Doris Page

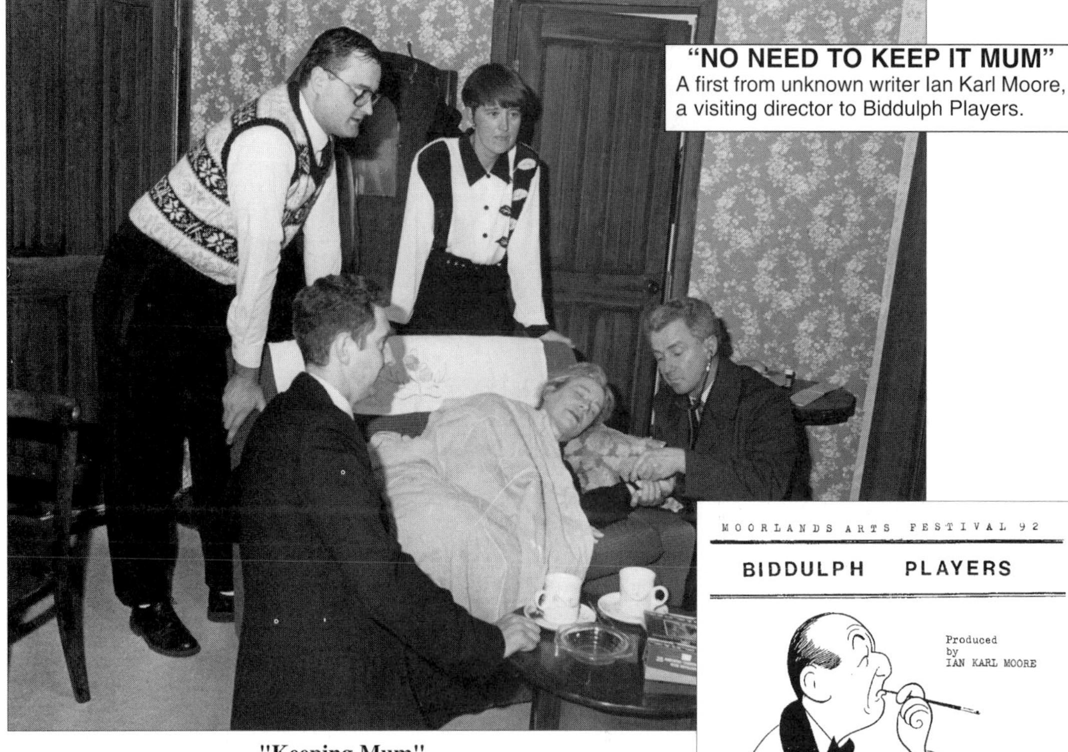

"NO NEED TO KEEP IT MUM"
A first from unknown writer Ian Karl Moore, a visiting director to Biddulph Players.

"**Keeping Mum**"
Ian Karl Moore, Hilary Hampton.
Leigh Colclough, Dorothy Murdoch, Peter Murdoch.

BIDDULPH PLAYERS

A COWARD COLLECTION

BIDDULPH TOWN HALL
Thursday 17 September 1992

Hilary Hampton

Hilary Hampton joined the Players hoping for a glamorous part. However, in the meantime she has played a middle-aged battle-axe, a punk girl-friend and an accident prone Felicity draped in blood soaked bandages.

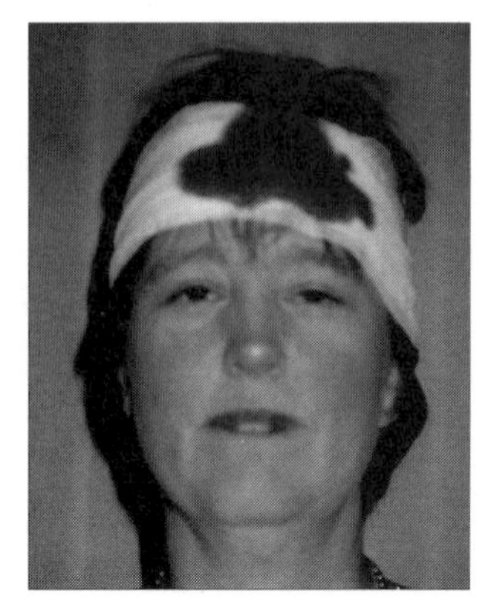

"ALL ACES IN PACK OF LIES"

A gripping play based on the true story of the Krogers, Russian spies convicted in 1961, and the shattered lives of their neighbours the Jacksons, caught up in a `pack of lies'.

"The star of Biddulph Players' production is undoubtedly Margaret Fernyhough, as Barbara - a perpetual worrier who becomes ever more distressed as she is forced to betray her friend.

Her portrayal shows a masterly grasp of mounting hysteria and self recrimination."

"Pack of Lies"
David Adey, Hilary Hampton.
Seated: Margaret Fernyhough, Dilys Johnson, Leigh Colclough.

"Blithe Spirit"
Dorothy Murdoch, Pat Gilman.
Mark Hurst, Bee Butler,
Doris Page, Melva Williams.

"SPIRITED PLAY ON UNFAMILIAR LINES"

The after dinner séance that goes drastically wrong when the first wife returns, causing mayhem.

"PRODUCTION OF "THE GHOST TRAIN" WAS ON THE RIGHT TRACK"

A delay causes train passengers to miss the last connection in this spooky drama by Arnold Ridley.

"Ghost Train"

Peter Murdoch, Hilary Hampton, Debbie Lovatt, Mark Hurst, Leigh Colclough, Kath Hallam, Paul Deane. Jonathan Hurst, Doris Page and Ken Tunstall.

Paul Deane

Grandson of Doris Page joined the society for the production of "Ghost Train" and also appeared in "The Late Mrs Early". We all hope he will remain with the Players carrying on the family tradition.

THE LATE MRS EARLY

Good Evening and welcome to our second play of the season its always nice to see familiar and new faces in our audience and we thank you for your support. There are two new faces in our cast for this production, Roger and Paul Deane making their stage debut, we wish them well.

Special thanks to all who helped in this production if you are interested in joining the players please contact any of the members on the door or telephone the secretary on 0260 226414.

We hope you have an enjoyable evening and have a safe journey home.

"BETTER LATE THAN NEVER"

Overbearing mother Alice returns as a vengeful ghost in this Norman Robbin's old-fashioned comedy.

"The Late Mrs Early"
Margaret Fernyhough, Rodger Deane, Alan Hart, Peter Murdoch, Dorothy Murdoch.
Seated: Dilys Johnson, Paul Deane, Debbie Lovatt.

"COMEDY ANOTHER SUCCESS FOR BIDDULPH PLAYERS"

Dennis makes a last ditch attempt to break away from the confines of his middle-class, housing-estate existence.

"One For The Road"
Leigh Colclough, Hilary Hampton, Liz Heap, Mark Hurst.

JUST WILD ABOUT WILDE AT BIDDULPH

Constance Cox's adaptation of Wilde's witty and improbable comedy. Lord Arthur has had his palm read and is told that he will commit a murder. He feels duty bound to get it over with before his marriage.

"Lord Arthur Saville's Crimes"
Dorothy Murdoch, Jonothan Hurst, Alan Hart, Ken Tunstall, Dilys Johnson, Peter Murdoch, Lisa Parr Brooks.
Seated: Leigh Colclough, Kelly Snape, Doris Page.

Costume

Costume plays are popular with actors and audiences but very expensive - often £20-£25 an outfit. The action of "Lord Arthur Saville's Crimes" takes place over several weeks necessitating four costume changes for many of the characters! We decided to hire one outfit per actor and then to either make the others or revamp them from our own wardrobe.

Acquiring satin, brocade and net from jumble sales served admirably, and charity shops were scoured for ladies' gloves, hats and trimmings. Then the three wardrobe mistresses all worked together, in a scene reminiscent of the "House of Elliot", to turn materials into outfits fit to grace Lady Windermere herself.

Leigh Colclough

"Leigh Colclough is in fine comic form as the bumbling Lord Arthur.

"CURTAIN UP AGAIN"

"In this wickedly amusing play Harriet solves her financial problems by entertaining two married gentlemen on different days of the week."

Producing

Casting can be the worst part of producing amateur drama. "Lord Arthur Saville's Crimes" was a wonderful play to produce and I was extremely lucky in having such a talented cast.

At the play reading it was fully cast, something which, as anyone connected with amateur productions knows, is nothing short of miraculous.

"Key For Two"
Hilary Hampton, Ken Tunstall, Rodger Deane.
Dorothy Murdoch, Peter Murdoch, Margaret Fernyhough.

"ALL HUMAN WORKING LIFE IS HERE"

"Stringer's Last Stand". Old fashioned comedy set in a the working class home of the Stringer family.

"Stringer's Last Stand"
Pat Gilman, Ken Tunstall, Leigh Colclough, Debbie Lovatt.
Seated: Jonathan Hurst, Liz Heap.

"Run For Your Wife"
Ken Tunstall, Leigh Colclough, Steven Shufflebottom, Robert Pope,
Peter Murdoch, Margaret Fernyhough, Dorothy Murdoch, Tim Hampton.

"AN EXCELLENT STANDARD SET BY PLAYERS"
Ray Cooney's highly amusing tale of the deceitful life of taxi driver, John Smith, who desperately tries to juggle his life between two wives.

"SECOND TIME ROUND FOR A CONFUSING AFFAIR"
Alan Ayckburn's comedy of infidelity and confusion in the lives of two couples.

"Relatively Speaking": Leigh Colclough, Dorothy Murdoch.

Peter Murdoch

Dorothy Murdoch

"PLAY IT AGAIN...... "

`Casting' back minds twenty years, amateur actors Dorothy and Peter Murdoch have got a case of déja vu in their latest production. For the couple are playing in the same play `Relatively Speaking' they performed in twenty years ago. The comedy has a cast of four, a young couple and an older couple. This time Dorothy and Peter are performing the role of the older couple in the production. Peter said "When we did the play before, we lived in Essex and we played the young couple then. It is surprising how many lines, even after all those years, are still familiar."

The society won three awards for this production. The Harold Horton Memorial Trophy for best actress was won by Dorothy Murdoch, The John Goldsmith Memorial Trophy for best play and the John Smith Memorial Rose Bowl for best stage production.

"LAST TANGO BROUGHT TALENTS TO THE FORE"

Mike Harding's acute study of a group of working-class, middle-aged northerners, setting off on their annual jamboree to Whitby.

"Last Tango in Whitby"

Debbie Lovatt, Robert and Anne Pope, Darren Brookes, Lee Westwood, Lucy Botham, Elizabeth Lawton, Irene Amos, Jose Frisby, Doris Page, Dorothy Murdoch, Liz Heap, Alan Hart, Betty Tittle, Pat Gilman, Peter Murdoch, Andrew Murdoch.

Anne Pope - subscriptions secretary

"Credit must go to Anne Pope, whose character was a typical reflection of a middle-class ballroom dancing has-been, trying to eke out a living on the hotel entertainment scene and loathing every minute of it."

Lighting

John Gilman

Of the venues in Biddulph the stage at Knypersley First School has the best lighting facilities, second only to the studio theatre at the High School - never considered suitable for the Players due to its location and restricted availability. It has not always been that way however. When the players moved from the Bateman School in 1971 to Knypersley First School the lighting facilities consisted of three ancient rheostat dimmers, two very dim spotlights and six low-powered floodlights. The main source of lighting came from the two overhead 300watt general purpose lights which had the effect of reducing the actors' eyes to black pools. Facial expressions are essential for conveying mood and feelings, and wasted if they can't be seen.

An interest in photography, and a desire for us to be seen, made me determined to sort things. Expensive, purpose-built equipment was out of the question. My first shot was to persuade the committee to invest in some additional 'real' theatrical lanterns and to botch up some domestic dimmers to improve the control. By replacing the control knobs with plastic gearwheels it was possible to obtain a crude simultaneous dimming of more than one circuit. With two banks of dimmers differential lighting effects could be obtained, however there were two problems. Firstly the dimmers had to be mounted close to the mains supply behind the set so the effect was not visible to the operator. Secondly domestic dimmers do not fade progressively but reach a low point then suddenly switch off - no good for a smooth operator.

This system however served the players reasonably well for a number of years until in 1983 I came across a couple of enthusiasts, Messers Garwell & Jamieson, who had experienced the same problems at Alsager. This pair had combined their artistic and electronic skills to develop and manufacture printed circuit boards which with some DIY could be built into a reasonably sophisticated lighting control system. After a lot of arm twisting at committee meetings, I finally got the go ahead - and more importantly the cash. The improvement was immense with full fade to black level, the ability to pre-set and cross fade between scenes and most importantly remote control. It even had a sound to light circuit which was used to good effect for Pat Moore's performance as a roller skating disco dancer in one of the 'Farndale Avenue' productions. An even greater asset at this time was recruiting Stuart Shingler. Adding the finishing touches well after midnight following the Sunday dress rehearsals was not uncommon. The stage at Knypersley First school is somewhat unique in having a ceiling which is only eighteen inches above the top of the proscenium arch and in fact lower than the ceiling in the hall. It is almost impossible to get the angles right in order to avoid shadows on the back drops especially behind windows. The silhouette of an actor against the sky is not conducive to a sense of realism; its no wonder I've lost most of my hair.

Never satisfied with the number of lanterns at our disposal, help came from an unexpected source; the desire to experiment with theatre in the round by the first school. Since this form of presentation needed lighting from three sides, three times the number of lighting units was required - an opportunity to raid the social fund yet again!

My work over the last seven years has made it impossible for me to be an active member of the Players but I understand that the lighting system has seen further improvements due to the enthusiasm of the current Headmaster. I miss getting involved - I'm just waiting for retiremental to arrive and I shall be back.

"PLAYERS SUCCEED IN FLUFFING THEIR LINES - ON PURPOSE"
A sinister, spine-chilling mystery of murder and mayhem performed by the Farndale Townswomen's Guild.

"Haunted Through Lounge"
Dorothy Murdoch, Paula Nixon, Debbie Lovatt, Katie Harrod. Pat Gilman, Dilys Johnson.

"TRAMPING OUT OF TOWN"
A one act play by Charles Mander.

"Shop For Charity"
Elizabeth Lawton, Anne Pope, Kath Hallam, Irene Amos, Dorothy Hibbitt, Robert Pope, Doris Page.

"LOTTERY COMEDY FOR PLAYERS"
A lottery win for Maurice and Jean and the disastrous effect it has on their lives, in this play by John Godber.

"Lucky Sods"
Betty Tittle, Peter Murdoch,
Hilary Hampton, Liz Howle.
Seated: Jonathan Hurst, Dorothy Murdoch.

Liz Howle

As well as being a familiar face on stage Liz has found time to take on another role vital to the Society. In 1999 she was elected secretary.

The first task she set herself was to contact local dignitaries and shop owners to invite them to become patrons of the Society. The response was very good adding many new names to the list in our programmes.

"BIDDULPH PLAYERS STAGE A DELIGHT"

An improbable tale of marital infidelity and confusion when three couples attempt to have an illicit weekend in the country.

"Will You Still Love me in the Morning"
Dilys Johnson, Peter Murdoch, Liz Howle, Ken Tunstall, Robert Pope.
Seated:
Mick McGregor, Alethea McCarthy.

Graham Bond

Graham has always been interested in drama and attended local performances but it was not until 1997 that he decided (with a gentle shove) to join the Players, a decision he has never regretted.

He intended to help with set construction, which he did on "Will you Still Love me in the Morning". He enjoyed the experience and happily went along to discuss the following production. He was rather surprised to be cast as the vicar and the waiter in "Confusions". Rather nervously he took to the stage and by the end of the production he was hooked.

He has since appeared in three more plays and assisted in backstage work, sound, lighting, set production, ticket and programme design.

"PLAYERS DID THEMSELVES PROUD WITH FOUR-PARTER"
Five inter-linked one-act plays which deal riotously with the human dilemma of loneliness.

"Relative newcomer, Graham Bond, who was a great help with the set building last time around, proved his worth as an actor in this performance, as a bumbling vicar unable to control the flow of tea from an urn."

"Confusions"
Graham Bond, Liz Howle,
Peter Murdoch.
Jonathan Hurst, Doris Page.

"Barraclough's Bounty"
Mick McGregor, Carole Willcocks,
Graham Bond, Liz Howle,
Ken Tunstall.
Seated: Dorothy Murdoch,
Robert Pope, Doris Page.

"TREASURY OF LAUGHS IN PLAYERS' BOUNTY"
Builder Charlie Barraclough finds a treasure chest in a house he is demolishing, in this northern 1970 comedy by Les Walker.

Bateman's Victorian Biddulph

Kath Hallam

When, in 1998, the Players were invited to organize a day for the first of the Festivals of Biddulph, the members set to with enthusiasm. Taking over the Town Hall for a whole day's activities meant a great deal of planning and work. From early morning all hands were employed in preparing a set of the drawing room of the Bateman household. Victorian games borrowed from Hanley Library, and the many historical artefacts were displayed for the exhibition. A group of the Players in appropriate costume took charge of the tearoom for the benefit of performers and public alike.

An upstairs room was requisitioned for Michael Pace, from the Newchapel Observatory, who gave shows of Victorian slides of the heavens with the aid of the epidiascope. Douglas Poole showed slides of the Biddulph Grange gardens; a panoramic confection of Victorian horticulture at its best.

Whilst preparations were nearing completion inside, street entertainers appeared on the High Street to draw in the crowds. And they came! The many visitors enjoyed the Victorian display; from a bassinet to a hip bath cabinet, from kitchen utensils to farm implements, from mining artefacts to a collection of polyphonic boxes. There was a wonderful demonstration of needlecraft and lacemaking by a group of local lacemakers, and in one corner there was a potted history of the town and notable characters, in words and pictures, all created on panels by Margaret Fernyhough.

Children were not forgotten. They looked in wonder, slightly bemused at first but ultimately enjoying the simple games of Victorian childhood; a far cry from the Game Boys of the 1990s. There was a magic show and traditional Punch and Judy to follow.

Graham Bond (Edward Cooke), Rob Pill (the Bishop), Peter Murdoch and Kath Hallam (Mr and Mrs Bateman)

The highlight of the day was an elegant carriage and pair which had bowled along the High Street from Biddulph Grange, coming to rest at the Town Hall steps. From it, to the cheers of the gathered crowds, stepped James and Maria Bateman (Peter Murdoch and Kath Hallam) and their guests, the Bishop (Rob Pill) and artist Edward Cooke (Graham Bond).

Members of the Staffordshire Regiment's Historical Section were waiting in their colourful uniforms of red, white and gold to present arms. The Bishop (Robert Pill), impressive in his purple and black, gave a short address to the citizens of Biddulph, bringing greetings from Queen Victoria herself. Moving towards the entrance, the Bateman party were greeted by the Butler (Robert Pope), Housekeeper (Doris Page) and a line of retainers before progressing into the hall itself. There they took time to enjoy the exhibition, chatting to all and sundry before proceeding to the Drawing Room.

Whilst the rest took their seats, James Batemen addressed the gathering. Then the audience watched as the Batemans were entertained in their Drawing Room with songs from Sheila Hood and poetry readings by members of the Congleton Writer's Forum. Afterwards the Butler served tea with cucumber sandwiches and slices of Victoria Sandwich.

Everyone who took part, even the co-ordinator (Tony Hall) and epidiascope operator, dressed accordingly. For a time, in the vicinity of the Town Hall, one could almost think that time had stood still.

Two hours sped by in a flurry of activity as the set, the Exhibition and tea room were dismantled to transform the hall ready for the evening's entertainment of an Old Time Music Hall. For this the services of The North Staffs Music Hall Association were called upon to augment our own and other local acts.

The Festival of Biddulph not only gives Biddulph a focus in July but also gives Biddulph Players an opportunity to diversify and try other things during our 'off season'.

Biddulph Players and guests waiting for the arrival of the Bateman family at the Town Hall.

Robert Pope - Chairman

Embarking on a new production is always a huge challenge and "Building Blocks", Robert Pope's first production, required a bathroom suite.

Before we could worry about the problems of man-handling it on stage and up a scaffold, we had to find one. We resorted to an Action Line appeal on Radio Stoke which resulted in a public spirited lady from Alsager offering us the use of one she had cluttering up her garage.

Our next worry was having a working cement mixer and piles of sand and gravel delivered on stage each night, and which had to be cleared afterwards ready for the next performance. By Sunday morning the cast and stage crew really felt that they had actually been working on a building site.

"Building Blocks"
Graham Bond, Peter Murdoch, Leigh Colclough.
Liz Howle, Ken Tunstall.

"AUDIENCE MUST PAY ATTENTION"

Another Farndale play within a play, a romantic 1930s comedy featuring characters based on Noel Coward and Gertrude Lawrence.

BIDDULPH PLAYERS A.D.S.

is proud to present the fourth collaboration with those lovely ladies from the

FARNDALE AVENUE HOUSING ESTATE TOWNSWOMEN'S GUILD D.S.

in

"We Found Love and an Exquisite Set of Porcelain Figurines Aboard the *SS Farndale Avenue*"

by David McGillivray and Walter Zerlin Jnr

Programme 20p

"SS Farndale"
Dilys Johnson, Graham Bond, Dorothy Murdoch, Hilary Hampton, Adrian Bemrose.

Alethea McCarthy

In 1996 Alethea discovered Biddulph Players. In her first play "Will You Still Love me in the Morning" she played Celia, a newly-wed, middle-class lady. It was a nerve racking experience to be first on stage and the first to speak.

The part required her to carried on by a lusty husband and as a finale, to strip down to her undies. To say Alethea had been thrown in at the deep end would have been an understatement!

It was harrowing, thrilling and at the same time exhilarating, but she was hooked - following an audition, Alethea will be seen on stage at the Shelton Rep theatre later in the year.

Income	
Sale of tickets	£559.00
Sale of teas	£ 57.60
Sale of programmes	£ 25.70
Sale of sweets	£ 3.64
Raffle	£ 94.90
	£740.84

Expenditure	
Raffle	£ 22.04
Ken (set)	£ 77.00
Wardrobe	£ 37.00
Tea	£ 8.07
Props	£ 15.00
Royalties	£168.00
Theatre licence	£ 14.50
Books	£ 64.44
Advertising	£ 43.24
Room hire	£127.17
Creative Signs	£ 41.12
N.S.D.A.adj fee	£ 51.00
Misc.	£ 10.00
	£680.58

Gross Profit on play	£60.26
Overheads (Clubroom)	
Gas	£ 63.63
Electricity	£ 17.15
Rates/Rent	£ 64.73
	£145.51
Net Loss	£85.25

Plays performed at

"PLAYERS HAVE FUN WITH FAMILY STRIFE"

This Ayckbourn time play opens and closes with a family's celebration of mother's birthday, at their favourite restaurant. Skeletons are revealed as the action moves between past and present.

"Time of My Life"
Leigh Colclough, Paul Deane, Ken Tunstall, Peter Murdoch.
Seated: Liz Howle, Alethea McCarthy, Margaret Fernyhough.

A Night at the Blitz

Frank A. Harris, Councillor

Friday 30th July, Saturday 31st July. 1999. Snapshot memories crowd back: Doris Page's delightfully dotty and whimsical Miss Willat; Robert Pope's larger than life yeoman farmer; Dorothy Murdoch, alias Dicky Tappe, struggling with a wilful false moustache as Enoch Blunt, plumber; the Home Guard and the stolid vertebra in the backbone of Old England; Alathea McCarthy as the sweet little gold-digger; the soft crooning of The Backroom Boys in the warm evening air in the courtyard as they waited to go on stage........

A Night at the Blitz was two nights staged at the Town Hall; two warm nights at the beginning of the holiday season, yet still two houses almost full to enjoy a mixture of monologues, sketches and songs recalling the darkest days of the Second World War.

Octogenarian Ben Leese launched the show with monologues from an astonishing anthology he has by heart, conjuring up the era just before the War. Then Edna Ferriday smouldered as Marlene Dietrich, and Mary Lloyd's clear evocation of The Forces' Sweetheart held the audience enraptured. John Whalley dazzled with his carefully-crafted tribute to George Formby - complete '*with his little ukelele in his hand*'. The Backroom Boys - a splinter group of the Biddulph Male Voice Choir - breathed life into Flannagan and Allen and a host of songs which had the audience joining in with many a misty eye.

As a 'guest director', the Biddulph Players made me very welcome. From first rehearsals I was taken aback by the professionalism of the Players, which saw actors dropping straight into character from the start, and meant that most of the cast knew their lines by the second rehearsal. Beyond the initial blocking, direction was hardly needed. It was soon obvious that the actors had a vast reservoir of experience and expertise.

The Town Hall showed its tremendous potential as a venue for this kind of production; accessabilty, ambience, comfortable seating and workable, if rudimentary, stage facilities.

Here's to the next fifty years!

"TIME OF YOUR LIFE" April 1999

"SEASON KICKS OFF TO A GREAT START"
An Agatha Christie spoof set in a country manor house in the 1930s, written by Peter Gordon.

"Murdered to Death"
Anne Pope, Peter Murdoch, Steven Bowers, Robert Pope, Leigh Colclough.
Seated: Hilary Hampton, Dilys Johnson, Liz Howle, Doris Page, Paul Deane.

"Tiramisu". A new play written by a local author, set in a small Italian Hotel.

"Tiramisu"
Ken Tunstall, Peter Murdoch, Ali Grinell, Simon Glynn, Dorothy Murdoch, Robert Pope, Liz Howle, Leigh Colclough, Graham Bond, Celia Richardson, Ali McCarthy, Hilary Stone.

All the Biddulph Players involved in "Tiramisu"
Back: Ken Tunstall, Tim Hampton, Peter Murdoch, Leigh Colclough, Graham Bond, Liz Howle, Robert Pope, Hilary Hampton, Simon Glynn, Ali McCarthy. Seated: Dorothy Murdoch, Ali Grinell, Celia Richardson. Front: Liz Heaps, John Skelding, Anne Pope, Kath Hallam, Margaret Fernyhough, Cath Gibson, Rob Pill, Amanda Stone, Shirley Fitchford, Doris Page, Elizabeth Lawton, Gladys Williams, Sheila Tunstall.

Sarah Wright

Our latest newcomer, Sarah is Ruby Birtle in "When We Are Married" and is also starring in "West Side Story" at Biddulph High School. We are always so pleased to see pupils involved with the Players - and just look at what happened to the 'Buxton' girls and Robbie Williams.

"When We Are Married"
Amanda Stone, Paul Deane, Robert Pope, Leigh Colclough, Ken Tunstall, Alan Hart, Graham Bond, Stan Sorby, Doris Page, Hilary Moss, Dilys Johnson, Kath Hallam.

Knypersley School

	TITLE	AUTHOR	PRODUCER
1971/72	"Ours is a Nice House"	John Clevedon	Doris Page
	"Waters of the Moon"	N. C. Hunter	Pauline McLellan
1972/73	"Sailor Beware"	P. King/F. Cary	John Ashton
	"Love in a Mist"	Kenneth Horne	Malcolm Haydon
	"Big Bad Mouse"	Philip King	John Ashton
1973/74	"I'll Get my Man"	Philip King	John Ashton
	"Strike Happy"	Duncan Greenwood	Malcolm Haydon
	"Relatively Speaking"	Alan Ayckbourn	Norah Cooke
1974/75	"Crystal Clear"	F. Cary/P King	Malcolm Haydon
	"We Must Kill Toni"	Ian Stuart King	Pauline McLellan
	"Brush with a Body"	M. McLaughlin	John Ashton
1975/76	"Time and Time Again"	Alan Ayckbourn	Malcolm Haydon
	"Friends and Neighbours"	Austin Steele	Malcolm Haydon
1976/77	"Milk and Honey"	Philip King	Melva Williams
	"The Late Mrs. Early	Norman Robbins	Malcolm Haydon
1977-78	"When We Are Married"	J.B. Priestley	Malcolm Haydon
	"Wolf's Clothing"	Kenneth Horne	Josephine Herbert
	"Wedding of the Year"	Norman Robbins	Josephine Herbert
1978-79	"Absurd Person Singular"	Alan Ayckbourn	Malcolm Haydon
	"Lloyd George Knew my Father"	William D. Home	Alice Ashton
1979-80	"How the Other Half Loves"	Alan Ayckbourn	Josephine Herbert
	"Tomb With a View"	Norman Robbins	Ken Tunstall
	"The Devil Was Sick"	Kenneth Horne	Alice Ashton
1980-81	"Two and Two Make Sex"	R.Harris/L. Darbon	Alice Ashton
	"Murder for the Asking"	Derek Benfield	Kath Hallam
	"Hobson's Choice"	Harold Brighouse	Alice Ashton
1981-82	"End of the Honeymoon"	Sam Bate	Alice Ashton
	"Portrait of Murder"	Robert Bloomfield	A.Vallely/K.Tunstall
	"Breath of Spring"	Peter Cooke	Alice Ashton
1982-83	"The Bride Comes Back"	Ronald Millar	Annette Vallely
	"Outward Bound"	Sutton Vane	Arnold Williams
	"Mock Orange"	Peter Blackmore	Alice Ashton
1983-84	"Off the Hook"	Derek Benfield	Alice Ashton
	"Barefoot in the Park"	Neil Simon	Ken Tunstall
	"White Sheep of the Family	L.du.Garde Peach/I.Hay	Annette Vallely
1984-85	"Ladies in Retirement"	E. Percy/R. Denham	Alice Ashton
	"Cure for Love"	Walter Greenwood	Ken Tunstall
	"Dark Lucy"	King and Bradley	Annette Vallely
1985-86	"Outside Edge"	Richard Harris	Ken Tunstall
	"Table Manners"	Alan Ayckbourn	Malcolm Haydon

1986/7	"Living Together"	Alan Ayckbourn	Malcolm Haydon
	"The Anniversary"	Bill Macilwraith	Dorothy Murdoch
	"Middle-Age Spread"	Roger Hall	Malcolm Haydon
1987-88	"Billy Liar"	K.Waterhouse/W.Hall	Dorothy Murdoch
	"Farndale Avenue Murder Mystery"	McGillivray/Zerlin Jnr	Peter Murdoch
	"Round & Round the Garden"	Alan Ayckbourn	Malcolm Haydon
1988-89	"There Goes the Bride"	Ray Cooney/J. Chapman	Dorothy Murdoch
	"Bedfull of Foreigners"	Dave Freeman	Doris Page
	"Time and Time Again"	Alan Ayckbourn	Malcolm Haydon
1989-90	"Taking Steps"	Alan Ayckbourn	Dorothy Murdoch
	"Our Day Out"	Willy Russell	John Gilman
	"They Came from Mars"	McGillivray/Zerlin Jnr.	Peter Murdoch
1990-91	"The Day After the Fair"	Frank Harvey	H. Moss/Ken Tunstall
	"Don't Start Without Me"	Joyce Rayburn	Leigh Colclough
	Ira Levin's "Death Trap"	Ira Levin	Dorothy Murdoch
1991-92	"Arsenic and Old Lace"	Joseph Kesselring	Dorothy Murdoch
	"Up 'n' Under"	John Godber	Dorothy Murdoch
	"Dear Charles"	Alan Melville	Leigh Colclough
1992-93	"Keeping Mum"	Ian Karl Moore	Ian Karl Moore
	"Pack of Lies"	Hugh Whitemore	Ken Tunstall
	"Blithe Spirit"	Noel Coward	Leigh Colclough
1993-94	"Ghost Train"	Arnold Ridley	Dorothy Murdoch
	"The Late Mrs. Early"	Norman Robbins	Leigh Colclough
	"One for the Road"	Willy Russell	Jonathan Hurst
1994-95	"Lord Arthur Saville's Crime	Oscar Wilde/C. Cox	Margaret Fernyhough
	"Key For Two"	J.Chapman/D.Freeman	Leigh Colclough
	"Stringer's Last Stand"	Stan Barstow/A. Bradley	Dorothy Murdoch
1995-96	"Run For Your Wife"	Ray Cooney	Leigh Colclough
	"Relatively Speaking"	Alan Ayckbourn	Ken Tunstall
	"Last Tango in Whitby"	Mike Harding	Dorothy Murdoch
1996-97	"The Haunted Through Lounge"	McGillvray/Zerlin Jnr	Peter Murdoch
	"Shop for Charity"	Charles Mander	Margaret Fernyhough
	(Stoke-on-Trent One-Act Play Festival at Mitchell Memorial Theatre)		
	"Lucky Sods"	John Godber	Leigh Colclough
1997-98	"Will You Still Love Me in the Morning"	Brian Clemens/Dennis Spooner	Dorothy Murdoch
	"Confusions"	Alan Ayckbourn	Ken Tunstall
	"Barraclough's Bounty"	Les Walker	Leigh Colclough
1998-99	"Building Blocks"	Bob Larbey	Robert Pope
	"We Found Love on the S.S. Farndale Ave"	McGillvray/Zerlin Jnr	Peter Murdoch
	"Time of My Life"	Alan Ayckbourn	Dorothy Murdoch
1999-2000	"Murdered to Death"	Peter Gordon	Dorothy Murdoch
	"Tiramisu"	Jack Axson	Ken Tunstall
	"When We Are Married"	J.B. Priestley	Margaret Fernyhough

Extracts From our Social Diary

Margaret Fernyhough

Before I put pen to paper, I thought it might be a good idea to look through the social committee minutes. Within a few minutes I was laughing out loud. The committee in 1982 were trying to organise a theatre trip and Doris was relating the story of a play she had been to see at Crewe, "Having a Ball". The play centred around a personal operation which one of our male members had just had and he volunteered to play the part (with feeling) should the Players consider putting it on. All this was recorded in the minutes by Cath because Sheila thought what fun it would be if anyone should read them in twenty years time.

Looking back through our records, I noticed how times have changed socially. All those dances, balls, gala nights and 'at homes'. On December 6th 1950 a dance was held in the Gymnasium, 5 shillings including refreshments, and a dinner dance at the Grand Hotel, tickets 10/6d. In 1953 dancing to Johnny Rex and his music, 6/6d including refreshments - proceeds to the flood disaster fund.

July 1st 1961 was a very memorable day in the Player's social calendar. Col. and Mrs W.A. Lovatt kindly gave permission for the grounds of their home at Spring House, The Hurst, to be open for a garden party. Special buses were organised from the Town Hall to arrive for the official opening at 3.00pm by Mrs C.W. Moreton. Admission was 1 shilling, and six pence for children, and the proceeds were to be shared between the British Legion, Darby and Joan and our own society funds. Events included donkey rides, a Punch and Judy show, a bonny baby competition and a display of dancing from the Mrs Rose Mountford School of Dance.

During the Bateman years, Alan and Mary Hart organised many social events, the venue being their own home. A wine and cheese evening with James Last, pie and pea supper with mini-auction, and a tramp's supper. On the menu was soup, jacket potatoes, sausage and beans. There was a prize for the best tramp; who won, I wonder? Alan remembers the evening well, having completely filled the Aga with potatoes, leaving no room for the heat to circulate, all the tramps eagerly awaiting their supper, and the potatoes uncooked!

As part of the Moorlands Festival we have played host to the ex-principals of D'Oyley Carte in concert at the Town Hall. These were excellent concerts and a useful boost to our funds.

We still have our theatre visits and Christmas and Summer walks, but our main events of the year are the Quiz Night, arranged by Graham, and the ever popular Mock Auction with everyone's favourite auctioneer, Leigh. He entertains us with two hours of non-stop jokes and banter. My favourite was the satin lined box he tried to sell as a coffin for a little budgie!

It is a lot of work for the social committee, but it is such an enjoyable evening and our main fundraising event.

Our social account is still called the 'Social and Building Fund' but dreams of having our own building perhaps have begun to fade. It pays for the upkeep of our clubroom and occasionally is used to subsidise plays in a bad season. We have just spent a great deal of money on two replacement heaters, reducing funds dramatically, but very necessary items when you consider that all our rehearsals and meetings take place during the colder months.

Dinner dance at the Biddulph Arms Hotel c.1961

Left: Rob Pill disguised as a tramp waiting for his supper.

Mushy Peas

1997 was the year of the 'mushy pea fiasco' for me. I had naively volunteered to cook the mushy peas for our annual pie supper, not anticipating the problems involved in cooking so many peas.

I failed to realise how many saucepans were needed or the fact they swell up four-fold. My whole kitchen at one time seemed to be full of peas, the slimy green, bubbling mass belching a green volcano down the sides of my cooker.

Mary Hart making a presentation to Doris Page after 35 years with the Players.

Our Annual Walks

The Players have had two organised walks each year for a long time now, starting from Doris's original Boxing Day wet Roaches walk.

We still have the annual Boxing Day walk and then an end of season walk in June/July - and of course we always end up in a pub or restaurant for a meal to put the weight back on again!

50th Anniversary

The 50th Anniversary Dinner Dance organised by the present Social Committee will be the grand finale for the year 1999-2000. We have tried to contact all past members and people are coming from far and wide to fill the Town Hall in Biddulph on the 6th of May.

Below:
Our annual mock auction with pie and peas supper is our main money raiser nowadays - Leigh Colclough provides the best entertainment of the year.

Bottom:
A splendid day out at the village of Eyam with a guided tour and lunch after at the Miners Arms.

PRODUCTION TEAM

Prompter........Amanda Stone
Set Designer........Ken Tunstall
Set Construction........Members of the Society
Stage Manager........Eric Frost
Lighting Designer........Graham Bond
Lighting & Sound........Chris Hurst & Tim Hampton
Properties........Anne Pope
Wardrobe........Margaret Fernyhough
Make-Up........Elizabeth Lawton & Dorothy Hibbitt
Front of House........Rob Pill and team
Refreshments........Sheila Tunstall and team
Fire Officer........Margaret Fernyhough

Biddulph Players A.D.S. Officials

President........Doris Page
Chairman........Robert Pope
Treasurer........Margaret Heap
Secretary........Liz Howle
Business Manager........Hilary Hampton
Subscriptions Secretary........Anne Pope

PATRONS

Mrs Bowcock, Mr. & Mrs A. Dale, Mr & Mrs A. Rushton
Mr & Mrs D. Fletcher, Mr. F. Hulme, Mrs E. Pepper
Mr & Mrs H. Moss, Mrs. F. Stoddard, Mrs D. Stubbs.B.A.
Mrs B Unwin, Mr S. Collier, Mr F. Harris, Murrays Travel
Mr J. Pedley, Mrs J. Connor, Hargreaves Opticians
Cllr E. Meredith, Cllr Brown, Cllr J. Ganon
Cllr J. Redfern, Mr & Mrs R Deane
Dr Eardley & Partners,
The Meadows School

LIFE MEMBERS

Mrs. G. Williams
Mr. & Mrs H Page
Mr. & Mrs. R. Pill

WELCOME TO OUR PRODUCTION

Those of you who support us regulary will notice some new faces in our midst. We would like to welcome Ali Grinell, Celia Richardson and Simon Glynn to Biddulph Players. We wish them well and hope that they keep in contact with us and appear in future productions.

A special mention must be made of another newcomer, Jack Skelding, the author of the play. Jack lives locally and has been very involved with the production of his play, and who knows, in the future we might produce another of his plays!

The year 2000 is very special for Biddulph Players as it is our 50th Anniversary year. Later in the year a book is to be published detailing the history of the Society, price £9.95. The launch date is to be May 6th and will be in the Council Chambers of the Town Hall, Biddulph. Information about the book will be in the local press, so look out for details.

Recently Stan Lee, one of the Caretakers at Knypersley First School has retired. We greatly appreciate all the help and support he has given to the Society over the years. We would like to wish Mr& Mrs Lee a long and happy retirement.

We are always pleased to welcome new members to Biddulph Players. If you are interested in joining us please introduce youself to any member of the Society who will be very happy to help.

Many thanks to Great Mills D.I.Y. Store who have helped with items for the set.

WE HOPE THAT YOU HAVE HAD AN ENJOYABLE EVENING AND HAVE A SAFE JOURNEY HOME

Idle Thoughts of an Amateur Actor

As you stand in the wings and the warning bell rings and the butterflies flit in your tummy,
While the anthem is played and your nerves are all frayed and you're feeling as numb as a mummy,
You gaze at the wall and try hard to recall the lines you should start the scene on,
And you find the play which you loved yesterday, you are now not the slightest bit keen on,
While you get the words pat you lean on a flat and the whole wall sways this way and thataway,
And here's poor Don Dart who was ready to start now running about like Chris Chattaway,
But the danger is past and now at long last, the curtain is up, spotlights glaring,
And now you're on set you break into a sweat, and stick to whatever you're wearing,
Before long for some cause there's a terrible pause which seems to go on for ages,
And the prompt looks at you and you give the wrong cue and you've cut out nearly three pages,
Though the scene's a bit lame you press on the same and you feel that you're getting the gist of it,
You begin to feel fine - then comes your big line - and you make such a terrible fist of it.
At the end of Act 1 you really have fun when the time comes for changing the scenery,
You pick up your chair and collide on the stair with Prop and an armful of greenery.
While the change is progressing you're rapidly dressing and looking in vain for some powder,
And your wife comes to say that she's enjoying the play but couldn't you speak a little bit louder?
Though struck to the heart you take this in good part and give the next scene a real clouting,
The Producer comes back and says, You're all right Jack, but why the deuce are you shouting?
You feel a bit eased when the audience is pleased and yet - is that clapping ironical?
Then you don't have to doubt when the papers come out and you look at the Sentinel and Chronicle
But the play is the thing - let the dramatist sing - make really good use of your leisure,
Though you sometimes pause and think with some cause, "Need I suffer so much just for pleasure."

This poem was found pasted inside the front cover of Alice Ashton's scrapbook. We know that John circulated copies of this poem to various members. Did he write it himself?

PRESIDENTS

1951-1963	LT. COL. J.W.A. LOVATT
1964-1968	ARTHUR FRYER
1968-1970	A. E. WILSHAW
1970-1972	JOHN ASHTON
1972-1976	HAROLD BOTHERAS
1976-1978	JOHN DIXON
1978-1982	ALAN ELSMORE
1982-1995	ARNOLD WILLIAMS
1995-2000	DORIS PAGE

CHAIRMEN

1950-1955	ALFRED T. ROGERS
1955-1964	JOHN HEATH
1964-1968	PHIL PEARCE
1968-1970	JOHN HEATH
1970-1973	HARRY MORRIS
1973-1975	ROBERT PILL
1975-1978	ALAN ELSMORE
1978-1982	ALAN HART
1982-1990	ROBERT PILL
1990-1994	ALAN HART
1994-1996	KEN TUNSTALL
1996-2000	ROBERT POPE

'The Oil That Keeps the Wheels Turning'
A Thank You to the Arts Council and Our Local Authority.

During all these years there seems to have been no time when cash resources were not something of a problem for the Players. Funds were supplemented, particularly in the early days, by social events - most enjoyable and helping to bind members together. But still the expenses were never ending - rents to be paid, play royalties, advertising and set construction costs.

We are fortunate that support given annually by the old Biddulph Council (product of $^1/_2$d rate for the support of the Arts) was continued by Staffs Moorlands District Council. Representatives of a variety of local societies meet monthly in Leek to encourage the arts in the district, and to consider applications for financial help.

The support from the Arts Council over the years is most sincerely appreciated - grants for the purchase of lighting and sound equipment, renewal of flats, restoration and heating of the clubroom, new chairs, sponsoring of the D'Oyley Carte Principals for profitable concerts.

Our Social and Building Committee has not yet had much of an opportunity to get involved with bricks and mortar though now and then our thoughts have turned to the possibility of a real theatre to perform in. Congleton have done it most successfully! Perhaps a reaction is yet to come against the increasing flood of canned entertainment. There are so many people in Biddulph that we never see at our plays, so much undiscovered talent that could enhance our performances. Sufficient perhaps to encourage us some day to go for a lottery grant and get a brand new place built in Biddulph?